THE RADICAL NOVEL RECONSIDERED

A series of paperback reissues of mid-twentieth-century U.S. left-wing fiction, with new biographical and critical introductions by contemporary scholars.

SERIES EDITOR

Alan Wald, University of Michigan

BOOKS IN THE SERIES

To Make My Bread *Grace Lumpkin*
Moscow Yankee *Myra Page*
The People from Heaven *John Sanford*
Salome of the Tenements *Anzia Yezierska*
The Great Midland *Alexander Saxton*
Tucker's People *Ira Wolfert*
Pity Is Not Enough *Josephine Herbst*
Burning Valley *Phillip Bonosky*
The Big Boxcar *Alfred Maund*

The Big Boxcar

Alfred Maund

Introduction by Alan Wald

University of Illinois Press
Urbana and Chicago

THE BIG BOXCAR

Manufactured in the United States of America
P 6 5 4 3 2
This book is printed on acid-free paper.

Library of Congress Cataloging-in-Publication Data
The big boxcar / Alfred Maund ; introduction by Alan Wald.
p. cm.—(Radical novel reconsidered)
Includes bibliographical references and index.
ISBN 0-252-06754-1 (pbk. : alk.paper)
ISBN 978-0-252-06754-9 (pbk. : alk.paper)
1. Afro-Americans—Southern States—Fiction. I. Title. II. Series.
PS3563.A876B54 1999
813'.54—DC21 98-35208
CIP

INTRODUCTION

A Southern Rebel in Cold War America

Alan Wald

A RADICAL LIFE

The task of recovering southern left-wing writers excluded from literary history due to anti-Communist and other prejudices remains incomplete. Among the most extraordinary of the southern radicals still living who belongs in the front ranks of any such new history is Alfred Maund (b. 1923), a novelist from Louisiana and veteran of many years in the southern labor and civil rights movements. Maund, like a surprising number of other socialists from the South, retained his left-wing vews all his life.[1] He has remained a Marxist, although without party affiliation, and a defender of the Russian Revolution and of Cuba; among his friends have been Communists, Trotskyists, and other socialists. Under various names he published political journalism about the South in *The Nation,* the *Monthly Review,* and the *American Socialist,* and he wrote for the Federated Press, the news service associated with Communist-led trade unions. Unlike the many left-wing writers who left the South to launch their careers, Maund resided for his first thirty-five years in the Deep South, including during the worst of the cold war years, when he began his career as a novelist with *The Big Boxcar.*

Maund was born on 26 June 1923 in Jennings, Louisiana. He was the only child of Alfred and Edna Caffall Maund, who came, respectively, from Iowa and Illinois. His grandparents on both sides were emigrants from England. A middle-class family, the Maunds were comfortable among the many northern residents in Jennings. Alfred Maund Sr. was a public servant all his life, holding jobs such as postmaster, parish fair manager, chairman of the City Democratic Committee, chairman of the Parish Selective Service Board, official of the American Legion, and city clerk. He was able to afford these low-paying and often unpaid duties because of income from the rice crops and occasional oil lease on the family farm.

Maund's father accepted the racial status quo, but attempted to deal fairly with African Americans, trying to help them obtain decent utilities and ensuring that they applied for the veterans' benefits to which they were entitled. He had generations-long friendships with black families, lending money without charge for them to build or repair homes, to send children to college, and to pay for illness. In one instance he was the foreman of a jury that gave a life sentence to a black man accused of raping a white woman. In the context of the time this was taken as the equivalent of a not guilty verdict and a refutation of the accuser. Maund's mother conducted Sunday school at the Presbyterian church and ran the local USO as a volunteer during World War II.[2]

Even before he was a teenager Alfred began writing a novel he called "The Mummy's Curse." Another early project was a naive effort to transform *Lamb's Tales from Shakespeare* into plays. After graduating from the local high school Maund attended Tulane University. He received a B.A. (Phi Beta Kappa) and an M.A. in English in 1944 and 1948, respectively. During his undergraduate and graduate years he worked as a sports writer for the *New Orleans Times-Picayune.* From 1946 to 1948 he taught English at Tulane as a graduate teaching fellow, and he was an instructor in English at Tulane from 1949 to 1950.

In 1948 he married Dorothy Dodson, a Newcomb graduate several years older than he. Her first husband, Julius Woeltz, was a painter who introduced her to the radical communities of New Orleans and Austin, Texas. They had a son, Stephen, then divorced soon after. When Julius subsequently died, Alfred adopted Stephen.

Maund spent much of his career as a journalist (mostly labor journalism) while occasionally teaching. After three years' service in the U.S. Navy, in which he achieved the rank of lieutenant (jg), he worked as an editorial writer for the *New Orleans Item* from 1950 to 1952 and then as a copy editor for the *Louisville Courier-Journal* from 1952 to 1953. From 1953 to 1955 he was an associate professor of English at Livingston State Teachers College in Alabama. He spent a year copyediting for *The Nation* (1955-56) and then edited *Labor's Daily* (a strike newspaper for the printers' union in Bettendorf, Iowa) from 1956 to 1957. In 1957 he began working for the International Chemical Workers' Union, editing the union's newspaper and serving from Akron as its public relations director.

In 1962 Maund took a leave from the union and for fifteen months he and Dorothy resided variously in the Caribbean, England, and France. When he returned to the union in 1963 he became a special projects writer, living in Washington, D.C. During that time he also served as the Washington correspondent and as a columnist for the Madison, Wisconsin, *Capital Times.* Dorothy, a professional social worker, obtained a job as the administrative assistant of Women's Strike for Peace, an important left-wing, antiwar organization.[3] In 1968 he and Dorothy were disgusted by the atmosphere in Washington caused by the Vietnam war and outraged by the drafting of son Stephen. So he answered a want ad and became an associate professor at the College of Petroleum and

Minerals in Dhahran, Saudi Arabia, a position that gave him and Dorothy an opportunity to travel around the world. They returned to the United States in 1972, and for the next seven years they cultivated citrus in Harlingen, Texas, in the Rio Grande Valley. Since 1980 he has been retired and living in New Orleans. Dorothy died of lung cancer on December 4, 1994, in New Orleans.

The origin of Maund's radical politics lies in his youthful observation of southern racist brutality in his hometown. Fascinated by John Brown at an early age, Maund later signed articles with the pseudonym used by Brown, Shubel Morgan. One long passage from Brown's speech to the jury that sentenced him to hang particularly influenced Maund:

> Had I interceded in the manner which I admit, and which I admit has been fairly proved . . . had I so interfered in behalf of the rich, the powerful, the intelligent, to the so-called great, or in behalf of any of their friends, either father, mother, sister, wife or children, or any of that class, and suffered and sacrificed what I have in this interference, it would have been all right. Every man in this court would have deemed it an act worthy of reward rather than punishment.
>
> I say I am yet too young to understand that God is any respecter of persons. I believe that to have interfered as I have done, as I have always freely admitted I have done, in behalf of His despised poor, I did no wrong, but right. Now, if it is deemed necessary that I should forfeit my life for the furtherance of the ends of justice, and mingle my blood further with the blood of my children and with the blood of millions in this slave country whose rights are disregarded by wicked, cruel, and unjust enactments, I say—Let it be done.[4]

This perspective and creed has strong implications for Maund's career as a novelist and as an activist.

At Tulane Maund was influenced by radical and pro–New Deal professors. These included Howard Palmer Johnson, who taught American history; Leonard Fellows Dean, who taught English literature; and Robin Feild, dean of the Newcomb Art School, who was born in England and considered himself a follower of Gandhi. Dorothy became Feild's secretary, and through Feild the Maunds met James A. Dombrowski, director of the integrationist Southern Conference Educational Fund (SCEF).[5] By the time Maund graduated from Tulane, his main interests were labor matters and "the black downtrodden."[6] Maund soon began to edit SCEF's monthly bulletin, the *Southern Patriot,* and Dorothy also went to work for SCEF.

As a student Maund had not been politically active but he was enlightened by leftist ideas. During his military service he continued to meet and talk with liberals and to read radical materials. His connections to the radical movement intensified during his 1952 stay in Louisville, where he encountered Carl Braden (1914-75), who had worked for left-led CIO unions and Henry Wallace's Progressive party campaign. Soon after, Maund started writing for *The Nation* on race issues; although he asked the editors of *The Nation* not to use his name, they persisted in doing so, which probably cost him his job at the college. Maund went to work as a copy editor for *The Nation* at its Alabama printing plant at the time of the Montgomery bus boycott. In Montgomery the Maund house became a center for visitors from the North who had come down to observe the boycott.

By this time Maund had become a socialist and he was attracted to the Soviet Union,[7] but he remained friendly with supporters of all the various Marxist currents and continued to collaborate on antiracist, pro-labor, and civil liberties campaigns with liberals. Farrell Dobbs, a leader of the Trotskyist Socialist Workers' party (SWP), was a guest in Maund's home on several occasions. Maund met him in a courtroom during the Montgomery bus boycott. They hit it off and began to socialize. Some weeks later another SWP leader, Fred

Halstead, arrived at Maund's door and introduced himself as a friend of Dobbs named "William Bundy." The Maunds fed and housed "Bundy," and together they interviewed E. D. Nixon, the boycott leader. (Maund's account appears in the April 1956 issue of the *American Socialist.*) Maund later met SWP members Ed Shaw, Rita Shaw, George Breitman, George Weissman, and Harry Ring.[8]

However, Maund did not like to be called an "independent radical": "It seems to cast aspersions on organized Marxists. I have sympathies with them all."[9] His basic view was that "the brotherhood of the working class is an objective proposition like the fact that the sun will rise tomorrow."[10] Maund contributed, always using pseudonyms for self-protection, to Marxist journals such as *Monthly Review* and *American Socialist,* but under his own name he also wrote articles for liberal publications such as *Frontier, New Statesman,* and the *Chicago Jewish Forum.* After World War II he read the Communist journal *Masses and Mainstream.* In the late 1950s the SCEF published his booklet, *The Untouchables: The Meaning of Segregation in Hospitals,* which was illustrated by Ben Shahn.

The Maunds were frequently red-baited for their activism, especially at the height of the Montgomery bus boycott. At the time Maund wrote an article for the Federated Press that was reprinted in the *Daily Worker.* This brought the wrath of the *Montgomery Advertiser* down on the Maunds in the form of an article denouncing Alfred for having Communist associations. Dorothy immediately lost all the advertisers to the newspaper she published at nearby Craig Air Force Base and she sued the *Montgomery Advertiser* for invasion of privacy. Her attorney was the noted New Dealer Clifford J. Durr. She worked in his office doing research to cut down on legal costs. SCEF supporters in New York held benefit parties. The suit, however, went nowhere; it turned out that the judge in the case was a regular columnist for the *Advertiser* but refused to recuse himself. Before Durr could file an appeal in a higher court *The Nation* closed its operations in Montgomery and the Maunds had found a new job that took them north to Iowa.

Early in life Maund had strong illusions about the redemptive power of unions and the superiority of the North over the South. Thus he was shocked by the vociferous anti-Communism of the AFL-CIO during the cold war. Although he did not become cynical, gradually his dream of unions and the North as saviors faded. His favorite political maxim became "No enemies on the Left," which he attributed to the civil rights activist Carl Braden, and "Always fight the bosses," which he attributed to the left-wing journalist I. F. Stone.

In the early 1960s two trips to Cuba convinced the Maunds to become unshakable Fidelistas. They defended the Cuban revolution in the *Akron Beacon Journal.* In the 1990s his views have not changed: After all, "There are still bosses," he notes.[11]

Although "race" has always been a central concern of Maund, he did not live among blacks. At an early age he was shocked by the treatment of African Americans and later became engrossed in black life and culture as he wrote for various labor, liberal, and radical publications. He began to consider devoting his literary skills to giving voice to black political and cultural resistance.

Maund's literary passion was fueled by his activism. During the Montgomery bus boycott the Maunds and two other couples were the only whites in the city who actively supported the boycott. Maund reported on the boycott for *The Nation.* He also did a substantial amount of work on behalf of the SCEF. The 1954 incident in Louisville, Kentucky, when Carl and Anne Braden bought a home in a white neighborhood and sold it to a black family became one source for Maund's first novel. The Bradens were charged with conspiracy to plot insurrection. Maund brought the case to the attention of the SCEF leader Jim Dombrowski, who helped raise bail for Carl Braden and who subsequently hired the Bradens as SCEF organizers. Maund wrote an article on the Braden case for the 8 January 1955 issue of the *New Statesman.*

THE ANTIRACIST IMAGINATION

Maund did not have a specific literary model for his novels; rather, he worked from the inspirations of wide reading, including works by some of the major leftist literary figures in the United States. Of Upton Sinclair's *The Jungle* (1906) he thought especially highly, and he read novels by both John Steinbeck and Nelson Algren. At Tulane he had read Lillian Smith's *Strange Fruit* (1944), a novel about black-white relations in the South, and thought it profound; Billie Holiday's song with the same name was a household anthem for years. He also read a great deal of Langston Hughes's poetry, although none of his fiction. For the rural episodes in his first novel Maund mined some of the same sources as had the young Erskine Caldwell.

During World War II Maund read Howard Fast's novels and considered Fast the most influential leftist novelist in the United States. *Freedom Road* (1944) along with *Citizen Tom Paine* (1943) and *The American* (1946) were provided him by the navy, which apparently saw propaganda value in their Popular Front patriotism. These books kindled Maund's democratic fervor. From Fast he learned the basic technique of trying to depict triumph against great odds. The poet Don West's sister, Jane, worked as Howard Fast's secretary, and it was through her that Maund initially made contact with Fast. Fast got Maund his first literary agent, which resulted in the publication of his first novel. Later, while Maund was teaching in Alabama, Fast asked him to sell copies of the novel he published himself, *Spartacus* (1952), upon his release from prison for refusing to disclose names of his political associates to McCarthyite witch-hunters.

Yet despite his admiration for the work of other novelists, Maund's writing is distinctively his own. *The Big Boxcar* (1957) is a masterful contemporary reconfiguration of motifs from Chaucer's *The Canterbury Tales,* probing the complex intersections of class, gender, race, and folk culture in the Deep South. The novel grew partly out of Maund's experience teaching Chaucer at Livingston. In Maund's novel tales are told to pass the time by a group of African Americans who have sneaked aboard a train boxcar heading North.

The *New York Times* praised the book for its "unpretentious perceptiveness," remarking on Maund's ability to handle "his Chaucerian series of tales with technical assurance and an arresting command over figurative language."[12] The *Saturday Review* also noted his artistic sophistication: "Mr. Maund melds his theme and his characters so skillfully that you feel the book virtually wrote itself."[13] Langston Hughes commented favorably on the novel in several publications.[14]

As expected, the southern press was brutal: "Maund set out to prove that Negroes are essentially fine people, and Southern whites are essentially sadistic heels," and "the stories are depressing, crude—and most of them manage somehow to bring in sexual relations between members of the white and Negro races."[15]

The Big Boxcar got a reception in his Louisiana hometown that rather surprised an apprehensive Maund. The Indiana-born publisher of the *Jennings News* ran an eight-column banner on the front page, under which he printed a press release and photograph from Houghton Mifflin, the publisher. The editor was a close friend of Maund's father. But neither Maund's father nor his mother ever said a word about the book, and Alfred and Dorothy never had the nerve to ask them. For the most part, all their acquaintances were mute, although gossip circulated to the effect that Dorothy, the New Orleans Communist woman, had led Alfred astray.[16]

The Communist Party's *Worker* saw *The Big Boxcar* as "an addition to working class literature" treating "the common fight of Negroes and poor whites for freedom in the south." The reviewer went on to idealize the novel's characters as "Southern freedom fighters" who learn "the meaning of united struggle and perceive the promise of even greater solidarity."[17] Sales of *The Big Boxcar,* mainly in the North and in England, were sufficiently impressive that the novel was later published in a paperback edition.

The International (1961), Maund's second novel, is a monumental dramatization of the major forces shaping the southern labor movement of the 1950s. It also sold enough copies to go into paperback (as *Blood of a Lion*). The novel is based on the rise of Wick Simmons, an Alabaman, who works as an organizer for a union headquartered in Cleveland, Ohio. The story of Wick shares with Dos Passos's work a picaresque quality with rapid "on-the-road" movements, although it is much more deeply rooted in knowledge of the inner workings of the labor movement than any of Dos Passos's novels.

Maund's last book, *The Worthy Termites* (1961), reflects the author's experience during the Montgomery bus boycott. Its characters suggest Rosa Parks and Martin Luther King Jr. The novel has a grotesque humor reminiscent of Nathanael West. Its style superbly dramatizes Maund's long-standing theme of romantics battling intractable and disillusioning reality.

In all three novels Maund consecrated his extraordinary skill as a storyteller to antiracist and pro–working class values. His aim was not to excoriate the South; rather, his efforts were inspired by the need for social redemption of the region. This is heralded in the dedication of The Big Boxcar: "To our native Southland and all our brave friends there . . . from Dorothy and me."

The Big Boxcar: ANTS AMONG THE FEAST

Maund's original title for his novel was "Pilgrims from Hell." But his publishers proposed "The Boxcar," and Maund cajoled them to add the adjective "Big" to convey "some idea that these stories had wide application."[18] Moreover, the book was originally written in the first person with the African-American Sam as the narrator. Sam not only told his own story in the first person but he also told the other stories. Maund's editor, however, was unhappy with this approach and urged a complete rewrite. In the process Maund inserted much new material, including the Woman's story, which was originally a play.[19]

When queried about general literary influences on the novel, Maund explains: "You might say that in the *Boxcar* I was trying to romanticize the social perspective of the Black downtrodden. While sticking to realism as much as possible, I wanted, through diction and images, to portray guts, imagination, and heroism. . . . I used the literary tools of a largely white tradition in order to dramatize and make vivid the souls, so to speak, of the Black voiceless."[20] Maund downplays the influence of the content of Chaucer's work on his novel, seeing the structure of *The Canterbury Tales* as a convenient framework, but one that could have come as well from other sources. Still, it is difficult not to be struck by the brilliance of Maund's choice of Chaucer's literary vehicle.

Chaucer used the technique of the "frame story" in the sense that *The Canterbury Tales* is a single narrative within whose framework are told stories that are themselves separate and distinct narratives. Both Chaucer and Maund depart from the frame model in that their story is not merely a perfunctory vehicle but a story in itself. The frame used by Chaucer is a pilgrimage to the shrine of Thomas à Becket in Canterbury, a commonplace and pleasant sojourn in which members of all medieval English ranks and classes participated. Maund follows Chaucer in presenting the contrasting personalities among his company of travelers.

Both writers also use rude juxtapositions to link ostensibly disparate themes. For example, in Chaucer a courteous tale is told by a Knight, which is then offset by the vulgarity of the Miller's Tale. One tale is used to enforce an argument made by someone who interrupts another's tale or sometimes to ridicule an opponent in these exchanges. Chaucer's Wife of Bath's Tale, about how women should be in charge of a marriage if the marriage is to work, inaugurates a whole sequence of marriage tales. Maund uses analogous interruptions; one of his tales inspires several responses.

We find yet another crucial parallel between Maund and Chaucer in the selection of a character to host the proceedings. In *The Big Boxcar,* the Woman performs that role, with firmness and aggressive command. Both Chaucer's host and Maund's Woman stand up to the various interruptions. Maund's Woman is a black woman of "easy virtue" who offers her own tale that in turn recalls the Wife of Bath's Tale, since it is the longest and most complex.[21]

Like Chaucer's pilgrims, the passengers in the boxcar are going toward a destination, in this instance the North. Yet Maund's African Americans are also running away, and it is usually away from the law. While *The Big Boxcar* certainly has the narrative vitality and earthiness of *The Canterbury Tales,* the journey it depicts is hardly the "pleasant" experience that Chaucer celebrates.

There are other significant departures as well. Sam (the surrogate for the author) enters the narrative at the onset and assigns the other characters nicknames because he says that he cannot "make out people plain" in the shadows (1). In fact, the telling of their own tales, in their own words, will illuminate these subalterns of the South. At first the denizens of Maund's boxcar insist that they do not want to talk about themselves and will tell stories only about whites. However, the stories they tell inevitably become autobiographical, because their lives and their conditions are inextricably interwoven with whites. This powerful motif is brought to a climax by Sam's tale, the final one, which seemingly takes another tack. Sam commences by saying that his story is not about whites, but concludes by revealing that he is the son of a white man who raped his mother.

From the outset Sam, the first character we meet prior to the Woman's assumption of leadership, is skeptical of the other passengers' motives, including the Woman. His point of view requires special attention. His naturalist gaze upon the land gives rise to metaphors that reflect his consciousness and physical hunger. To him, the land looks like a picnic blanket. The landscape transforms into food images and he starts to play a fantasy food game. Gradually it dawns on Sam that blacks in the South are like insects at someone else's picnic, "ants among the feast" (2). The political implications of this image are powerful, especially when situated in the novel's setting—a group of blacks in a boxcar heading North, struggling to escape white racist domination. For historically conscious readers, this may invoke associations with the 1932 Scottsboro case, an international cause for the Left.

Sam's altruistic decency is established early when he raises his hand in a sign of hope to the black children whom he sees from the boxcar—the hope of escaping the South. He then intervenes on behalf of another passenger, Shorty, whom he regards as a naive country rube duped by city slickers. The Woman, too, is depicted early as having concerns broader than mere self-survival or, perhaps more accurately, as seeing self-survival necessarily bound up in group survival.

Another theme introduced early is that of "unmasking." The Woman first appears dressed as a man, an initial masking, which prefigures the later unmasking of Jonah's unintentional disguise as a black man. However, the change of the Woman's identity anticipates many altered perceptions that will occur as the boxcar travels northward. Maund's own role, as a white author depicting blacks telling stories about whites, encourages the introduction of issues of identity and ambiguity.

Maund's boxcar, therefore, holds great metaphorical potential. The train going North suggests the African-American spiritual "This Train Is Bound for Glory" as well as the Underground Railroad. Since the laws of the capitalist state do not obtain in the boxcar, a foundation exists for a new kind of egalitarian utopian order. The passengers choose their leader, the Woman, not because of her economic wealth but because of their assessment of her intelligence and courage. In a certain sense the boxcar becomes a relatively classless society in which none of its occupants has substantial material privileges. All discuss and choose; together they learn that they can gain their freedom through collective action.

The first tale told is the story of Good Rocking Poppa and his dealings with the white Dr. Morris. It begins in a manner recalling themes from Langston Hughes's *The Ways of White Folks* (1934). Poppa ridicules whites' eroticized fantasy of black life. Dr. Morris is on a search for what he imagines to be genuine African-American culture. However, the black night club to which Poppa directs him, the Elite Treat, is deceptive; it is a place not for ordinary blacks but for only the wealthiest stratum. Lula Blue, the black singer with whom Morris begins an affair, ultimately becomes inauthentic; she passes for white and dies. Dr. Morris, in self-defense, embraces a liberal explanation; he blames "society" for killing Lulu. But Poppa does not buy it. However, Poppa's revenge against Morris is as much a validation of his own manhood as a blow for civil rights. Consequently, it almost seems irrelevant as to whether Poppa was really Lula Blue's "brother," as he reveals at the end, or her symbolic brother.

As in *The Canterbury Tales,* a discussion follows Poppa's story. The Woman is the most dubious about the suggestion that perhaps the interracial couple might have found a place without racism to which to escape. Sam finds that he cannot be objective because he is jealous of the apparent mutual attraction between Poppa and the Woman.

Shorty's story, which comes next, has a country setting, enabling Maund to present the reader with a different black southern experience. Shorty introduces his tale by describing an economic and class configuration, in contrast to the more personal first story. His tale of the appearance of the Talking Dog (although based on a pointer once owned by Maund)[22] recalls West African "talking animal" stories, which were brought to the Western Hemisphere by slaves who passed them on, telling them to white children whom they raised. Thus the stories/parables entered the culture as a whole.[23] Shorty's Talking Dog advances the spirit of revolution because the dog is associated with union organizing and fighting the KKK. A proverbial "outside agitator," the dog has unusual markings that make him appear to be both a pirate and a clown. The dog also exudes masculinity by displaying its penis boldly, prefiguring the impregnation of Joe Dabbs's bitch bird dog at the end of the tale.

While the Talking Dog does not talk much, Shorty relates that it takes the measure of every man and is called a "voodoo animal" by the sheriff (27). Shorty speculates that the dog really can talk but refuses to as a sign of resistance. Ultimately, the dog functions to galvanize disparate individuals into a closed fist. This is the traditional role played by radical political organizations; it is the ultimate unity of the black comnunity that finally forces the sheriff to back down.

Teacher-Man's story is an amusing dramatization of the themes of agency and appropriation by the oppressed. Viewing the bizarre behavior of the white Major Carling, who wants to enlist him in a religious crusade, George Little is scared but stirred. He senses an opportunity to break out of the prison of routinized life. Earlier, George had been shamed into passivity by a black preacher; now he uses the crazy behavior of the white major to acquire what he perceives as new, liberating experiences. When he brings Carling before the black congregation in his church, he receives an ambiguous response; the young girls feel liberated momentarily and think that an outdoor revival will let them show off their finery; the elders hold back. In the end George has to run for it to escape a white mob. In miniature, the story may address contradictions in the adoption by African Americans of Christianity and other European-American institutions foisted upon them by the oppressor society. At first George happily abandons his "regular life" to participate in disruptive activities that enable him to break free of routine; yet, limited as it is by the cover of Major Carling, the rebellion is ultimately deceiving, and George, later revealed to be Teacher-Man himself, must set out on his own to master a more complex vision.

The Woman (who has revealed that her name is Marie) tells a story embodying a blues theme; it is a tale of forced promiscuity and all the painful details of her brutal oppression due to her race, class, and gender. Political concepts are brilliantly dramatized in the opening episode of Marie's arrest and mistreatment and that of her white girlfriend, Sarah. While blacks are born "criminalized," whites have to earn a criminal record before they are treated similarly. Yet when the two women are raped by the same policeman an element of common oppression of women of all colors in a patriarchal society is revealed. There is also the narrative of Marie's boyfriend, Alexander, who wanted to be a boxer and support Marie. He is symbolically emasculated when the police break his hand, and his dream of economic independence and dignity is smashed. He then gradually turns to pimping; this male exploitation of a black woman in response to the indignities of white racism recalls a theme frequently dramatized by Chester Himes in his novels.

Marie's story then suddenly switches to an absurdist atmosphere introduced by the two strange professors, Tatsumi and Hastie, who are trying to induce cats and rats to live harmoniously. They believe that a successful experiment with the animals will shame humans into acting more decently. Marie's political consciousness begins to expand. She casts off her ignorant stereotype of Asians. Initially she thinks that Tatsumi is Chinese, but he is actually a Japanese-American victim of incarceration in World War II detention camps in the United States.[24] She learns that his wife died in internment and that his son was killed while fighting in Italy with a U.S. combat infantry regiment. Tatsumi now becomes in her eyes "colored," "the same way she was colored—that is, not only skin-colored but *trouble*-colored" (73). Marie next recognizes that Hastie is becoming less "white" as he begins to purchase a home for Marie's relatives.

The Spook's story provides comic relief with its description of the three heads that pop out of his shoulders under the influence of marijuana. The heads articulate previously repressed feelings, and arguments break out among them. The Spook's interaction with the Jewish journalist, Mr. Kaplin, raises the issue of the ambiguous role that other religious and ethnic minorities play in the South.

Jonah's ribald story, which follows, dramatizes class differences among whites in the South. The family name in the story is Fluke, and at first it seems to Jonah that it is mere chance (a "fluke") that determines one's social fate. However, his tale reveals that it is greed and the corrupt pursuit of economic power that determine one's fortunes, right up to and including one's chances in court.

Jonah, who has been exposed as being a white man just

before telling his tale, manages to earn his place in the boxcar by his story, thereby avoiding being tossed out, as was his biblical namesake. His tale wins sympathy because it echoes various painful experiences shared by African Americans in his narrative of the theft of his money, the false rape charge against him, his imprisonment, and his desire to escape to the North. His experience resonates most strongly with the Woman, who is the most politically developed person in the boxcar; at her moment of reaching out to Jonah, she seems to embody Maund's own philosophy as expressed in *The Untouchables:* "Until men learn to love one another as brothers, pain, with its disregard for race and color, remains the strongest bond between man and man. Suffering is not competitive."[25]

In the final tale Sam reveals that he is the illegitimate son of the white, old, nearly senile Colonel Scruggs, who was assigned to spy on the female teacher in the black schoolhouse where Sam is the janitor. Sam had hoped to learn from the teacher, a light-skinned black woman, but it turns out that she is sexually repressed and wants him only to play the part of a primitive in her erotic fantasies. In the course of his narrative Sam finds that he is not "himself," that schools and teachers lie, and that one has to employ books for one's own ends. Finally, he burns the schoolhouse down and appropriates the idea of the newly learned word *nomad* to justify his departure.

The novel climaxes at Birmingham, where the Spook volunteers to become a decoy to distract the police and is killed. The Woman and Sam then leave the boxcar, and, after they successfully distract the police, they see an unidentified arm raised from the boxcar as a sign of solidarity. The pair confuse the police by using racist stereotypes against the racists; since whites need to believe that blacks are animal-like, Sam and the Woman act like animals, feigning sexual intercourse on the ground to assist their comrades' escape.

Here the Woman willingly sacrifices her "dignity" for the sake of the collective good. Sam's awareness of this, and his participation in a humiliating act of sexual degradation, results in a change in his consciousness. He comes to regard the sexual exploitation of his own mother and the Woman as externally imposed, rather than a flaw in their inner characters.

After escaping, Sam at first works as a janitor and the Woman finds a job as a teacher. He is studying welding and hopes to join a union. It is implied that the Woman will play a role in the coming civil rights movement. Although Sam's original goal was to reach the North, he concludes he can stay in the South but must carry out the progressive political activity that Maund has always associated with the North. The communal experience of the boxcar, and his bonding with the Woman, have transformed Sam so that he is able to forge new goals despite the oppressive Southern environment. Still, the novel's ending should not be read as unqualifiedly optimistic; Sam's aim of acceptance into such a racist outfit as the Building Trades Union of that time is yet another example of a romantic hope that will have to sustain itself against enormous odds.[26]

The Big Boxcar operates within but also substantially enhances the tradition of radical culture in the United States. It can be seen as an instance of "proletarian culture" that recycles the techniques of conventional high culture (Chaucer) to demonstrate that the ordinary experiences of black American life in the twentieth century are as worthy of literary expression as those of whites in medieval England. *The Big Boxcar* is also a vivid example of the radical genre of "bottom dog" literature,[27] one that accommodates black experience to that category. In *The Big Boxcar* all the characters have been cast from their home communities and are fleeing the law. Yet the intense oppression visited upon blacks by racism and capitalism in the South at that time brought a very large sector of the African-American population much closer to a bottom dog existence than was the case among the white working class at the height of the Great Depression. Indeed, there may not have been an authentic separation between southern black workers and the on-the-road characters in *The Big Boxcar.*

Alfred Maund extends the radical tradition of European-American writers by recreating the black struggle against oppression from a developed sense of identification, respect, and class perspective. His characters' efforts at cross-cultural representation—blacks telling tales about white characters—helps to legitimate Maund's effort to tell tales by black characters.

Significantly, in the final episode as the boxcar arrives in Birmingham, a white character appears who represents new hope in the struggle against the seemingly relentless oppression of blacks. At the moment of crisis in the railroad yard, after the boxcar has rolled on and the police are standing over the prostrate Sam and the Woman, threats begin to circulate among the whites present. There is talk of shooting or burning the helpless couple. Suddenly onto the scene comes another unnamed white man, apparently a railroad clerk. He makes it clear, by his questions and by his urging everyone to move on, that he personally will not cooperate in any sadistic brutality against the couple. The narrative voice observes:

> Sam didn't reason it through till a long time later, but he came to think how that railroad man's manner showed how a white man who doesn't like to see Negroes beat and killed can stop a good bit of it, and do it easy. He can just make it known he is ready to be a witness. He might not ever have to raise his hand and swear, he doesn't have to give a helping hand in big style. He just needs a steady eye. . . . The tiniest white man can shame off murder and bloodshed if he looks on and hints by not joining in that he doesn't agree. (174)

Like Jonah in his novel, Maund's being a white man makes him suspect as a reliable storyteller and fellow traveler, until some grounds for accepting him are established. Jonah knows that his task is to prove his common humanity with his fellow passengers on the journey, and he does this by revealing shared oppressions.[28] Although Maund's life of activism is eloquent testimony to his unbending commitment to social emancipation, his novel makes its bid as an instrument of black liberation through his use of consummate craftsmanship in offering us a literary "witness" to the structural racism of capitalist society that sets ordinary people of different colors against each other to the disadvantage of all.

NOTES

I am grateful to Patrick Quinn, Ellen Poteet, and Alfred Maund for their comments on a draft of this introduction.

1. The only real apostates among leftist southern writers were Grace Lumpkin (1892?–1980), author of *To Make My Bread* (1932; reprinted in 1995), and William Lindsay Gresham (1906–62), a Spanish Civil War veteran who specialized in books with carnival and occult themes. Both underwent religious conversions in the 1940s.
2. Letter from Alfred Maund to the author, 19 Jan. 1998.
3. See Amy Swerdlow's *Women Strike for Peace: Traditional Motherhood and Radical Politics in the 1960s* (Chicago: University of Chicago Press, 1993).
4. Quoted in Maund, "John Brown's Legacy," 313.
5. The Southern Conference Educational Fund was founded in 1946 in New Orleans to eradicate segregation. Although originally led by the New Deal liberal Aubrey Williams and sponsored by Eleanor Roosevelt, the organization was nonetheless mercilessly red-baited throughout the McCarthy era.
6. Letter from Alfred Maund to the author, 15 July 1991.
7. When he traveled to the Soviet Union and Eastern Europe in the late 1960s, he found that the difficult living conditions pretty much

matched his expectations. However, he was especially upset at the demeanor of the East German border guards. When he visited China after the Cultural Revolution he found it depressing, yet not as depressing as India.

8. Letter from Alfred Maund to the author, 9 July 1991.

9. Ibid.

10. Letter from Maund, 19 Jan. 1998.

11. Letter from Maund, 9 July 1991.

12. See Lee, "Fugitives En Route."

13. See Dempsey, "On the Lam."

14. See, in particular, Hughes, "Books for Christmas: 1957."

15. See Atkins, "Fiction on Integration."

16. Letter from Maund, 19 Jan. 1998.

17. Sanders, "Negro-White Unity in the Big Boxcar."

18. Letter from Maund, 15 July 1991.

19. Letter from Maund, 9 July 1991.

20. Letter from Maund, 15 July 1991.

21. However, while sex is employed manipulatively by the Wife of Bath, in the Woman's tale it is an instrument of domination through rape and forced prostitution.

22. Letter from Maund, 9 July 1991.

23. At first animal tales were invented to explain features of the universe, but then they evolved into entertainment and a form of instruction. In the planatation South the rabbit stories were especially effective at amusing while imparting wisdom by showing a trickster figure who outwits and gains mastery over stronger and more powerful forces. For example, Brer Rabbit is often seen as a stand-in for a slave.

24. During World War II Maund attended a Navy Japanese language school where the instructors had been given the choice of teaching or staying locked up in a concentration camp. Letter from Maund, 19 Jan. 1998.

25. Maund is referring to physical pain in this pamphlet about segregated hospitals. I am grateful to Jeremy Wells and Ihsan Taylor for drawing my attention to this passage.

26. Letter from Maund, 19 Jan. 1998.

27. See Walter Rideout, *The Radical Novel in the United States,*

1900–1954 (Cambridge, Mass.: Harvard University Press, 1956), 185.

28. For a number of these observations I am grateful to Jeremy Wells and his paper "The Other's Side of the Tracks."

BIBLIOGRAPHY

Selected Works by Alfred Maund

"Battle of New Orleans: Eastland Meets His Match." *The Nation,* 3 Apr. 1954, 281–82.

"The Braden Case." *New Statesman and Nation,* 8 Jan. 1955, 34.

"Deep South" (under the pseudonym A Correspondent in Alabama). *New Statesman and Nation,* 21 Aug. 1954, 203–4.

"Feathery Fable—A Tale My Uncle Remus Never Told Me." *Frontier* (Dec. 1955): 14–15.

"The Future Comes to the South." *The Nation,* 17 Jan. 1953, 47–48.

The International. New York: McGraw-Hill, 1961.

"John Brown's Legacy." *Monthly Review* (Jan. 1955): 312–22.

"Monster Rally at Montgomery." *The Nation,* 18 Feb. 1956, 2.

"The Negro Novelist and the Contemporary Scene." *Chicago Jewish Forum* 12 (1954): 28–33.

"New Day Dawning: The Negro and Medicine." *The Nation,* 9 May 1953, 396–97.

"New South, Old Sin" (under the pseudonym Shubel Morgan). *Southern Farm and Home* (Oct. 1953): 5.

"Peons on Wheels." *The Nation,* 14 Nov. 1953, 393–94.

"'Progress' in the South" (under the pseudonym A Special Correspondent). *Monthly Review* (Sept. 1953): 202–5.

"Prospects for Negro Educators." *Chicago Jewish Forum* 12 (1954): 160–61.

"Readin', Ritin', and Retooling." *The Nation,* 14 Mar. 1953, 2.

"Southern Schools: Will Racism Be Erased" (under the pseudonym A Special Correspondent). *Monthly Review* (Dec. 1964): 279–83.

The Untouchables: The Meaning of Segregation in Hospitals. New Orleans: Southern Conference Educational Fund. Undated pamphlet.

"Walking Their Way to Freedom" (under the pseudonym A Special Correspondent). *American Socialist* 3.4 (Apr. 1956): 9–11.

"We Will All Stand Together." *The Nation,* 3 Mar. 1956, 2.
"Which South Do You Mean?" *Chicago Jewish Forum* 13 (1955): 26–29.
The Worthy Termites. London: Longman's, Green, 1961.

Reviews of The Big Boxcar

Atkins, J. "Fiction on Integration." *Louisville Courier-Journal,* 13 Oct. 1957, sec. 6, p. 4.
"*The Big Boxcar.*" *Kirkus Reviews* 25 (1 Aug. 1957): 549.
Bloom, Beryl. "Under the Club." *Contact* (Capetown, South Africa), 18 Apr. 1959, 14.
"Briefly Noted." *New Yorker,* 12 Oct. 1957, 197–98.
Caughey, John. "A Birmingham Tale." *Frontier* (Nov. 1957): 17.
Dempsey, David. "On the Lam." *Saturday Review of Literature,* 12 Oct. 1957, 27–28.
Emery, Lawrence. "Life in the Deep South." *National Guardian,* 30 Dec. 1957, 4.
Halstead, Fred. "The Big Boxcar." *Militant,* 11 Nov. 1957, 4.
Hughes, Langston. "Books for Christmas: 1957." *Chicago Defender,* 21 Dec. 1957, 8.
Lee, Charles. "Fugitives En Route." *New York Times Book Review,* 5 Oct. 1957, 39.
Sanders, Don. "Negro-White Unity in the Big Boxcar." *Worker,* 27 Oct. 1957, 4.
Saxton, Alexander. "Birmingham Tales." *American Socialist* (Mar. 1958): 23.
"Shades of Meaning." *Times Literary Supplement,* 13 Feb. 1958, 28.
Stallings, Sylvia. "Six Modern Pilgrims Going to Birmingham." *Houston Post,* 6 Oct. 1957, 9.
Watts, Hilda. "Six on the Run." *Fighting Talk* (Johannesburg), (Apr. 1959): 13.

Other Sources

Wald, Alan. Interview with Alfred Maund. New Orleans, La., Nov. 1989.
Wells, Jeremy. "The Other's Side of the Tracks: Alfred Maund's *The Big Boxcar* and the Politics of Cross-Representation." Essay for graduate seminar at the University of Michigan, Apr. 1995.

The Big Boxcar

To our native Southland
and all our brave friends there
. . . from Dorothy and me

THE TRAIN was moving slow — just as Sam had seen it do when he was hitching Jess the mule on many a morning at plowing time. The dawn sun shone splashy red like a pullet egg, and the soil was brown-wet as a man could ask. But Sam wasn't looking at things from behind a mule's ass. He climbed aboard, just him and a bundle, saying goodbye to Lauderdale County, Mississippi. Heading North.

Sam made the sixth in the boxcar. And though he was a country man who never left his house of birth more than thirty miles any direction, he knew it bad for six black men to be coveyed close like this. One Negro boy a policeman finds can beg and crawl and get off with a kick and a cussing. But more, and white policemen reach for their guns, and Negroes together don't want to be the first to kneel. Death and bloodshed.

The others in the car knew it, too, Sam could tell by their eyes, but this was the only open car he could have caught on. They must have appreciated that, because they didn't speak; they sliced him a share of their slim chance without a word.

The car was too shadowed to make out people plain, but from a sneaky look-around Sam decided they weren't of a party. Each had made his own choice; each had his private trouble.

They rolled along in quiet an hour or more. Sam watched the land, from habit's sake, and saw it spread out like a picnic blanket, all colors and lumps. At one place somebody had eat his fill and left just toothpick pine and clay gulleys the color of spilled catsup. He'd eat his fill and gone. More than one had got his belly full and gone. Then one big pasture, miles long, green — green like good pea soup with cows floating around like salted crackers — *there* somebody was eating still. He played the food game a long time, comparing what he saw to a holiday meal, because he wanted to give his leaving day a happy feel. What was more, all that outside was the same as that he'd left behind and he had to make it seem new so he could feel he was on his way.

A fine field, just dug up, came by, black and deep, like chocolate cake. Like a cake. Sam laughed at his own smartness, until smack beside the rails was a shanty made into a house out of an old cotton storehouse. It gave him a sore turn. He knew every crack in that red-sided two-roomer which had a ramp running down one side instead of a porch, and could guess within four-five how many rats there was; it was the spit-image of the home he'd left. Two little children stood on the ramp, waving their hands — little rag-tags pumping halloos at every car that passed. They smashed his picnic mood.

What are we but ants among the feast, we Negroes? We are the feasters' joke that makes their food taste better even while they fuss and tread us under foot. Just ants! Sam thought all this, and hot with the thought he leapt up and stuck his head out and waved back to the kids. He knew it a foolish thing to do, to risk an unfriendly eye. But he wanted to say "Look at me! Look at me!" to those kids and point the way a man must go when he's grown. He made a big wave, even if inside he couldn't tell whether he was leaving them behind or they were leaving him.

"Sit down, fool!" a big voice said. Sam sat, scrunched back in a corner of the car, all to himself. The floor was hard and damp. Spilled grain ate through his jeans like buckshot. Nothing happened for a while until the train made a turn that let more sun into the car, turning the shadow to mustard-gray.

Then, like a fat old hen getting off the nest, one of the people across from Sam stirred himself and stood up. He moved to the center of the car and started dusting himself, showing off his black-stripe suit. Sam was impressed by the woolly white felt the man had on; except for some patches of grease stain it was razor-sharp. The man was baggy built, but he held his back stiff and his belly out, and his bottom lip and eyebrows drooped like they were weighing a bale of important plans. He scuffed around in a circle, rocking more than the train called for. He reminded Sam of a honky-tonk owner he had seen once, so to himself Sam named him Good-Rocking Poppa, for the fun of it.

"Who's got an old blanket?" Good-Rocking Poppa said suddenly, like a general calling for a horse. Nobody gave reply. He wrinkled his flat nose up and down and lit a cigar that wasn't more than half used. "Now look here, gentlemen," he said again. "I'm a gambling man of more than usual luck. It wasn't bad luck brought me here, it was good. They was watching all the Pullmans and buses." He gave them a minute to guess who *they* was. "I still got luck to burn, and I was wondering if any of you sports wanted to try put out the fire." He held out his hand, and sitting on the palm was a pair of dice. He flipped one up in the air and caught it, then hunched there waiting.

"I got a blanket and a mite of risking money," a real short fellow said, moving up like he was on hands and knees. He slung a gray blanket to the floor and started unknotting a handkerchief he pulled out of his blue jeans. Old Shorty looked more like a bull pup than a gambler; he didn't appear to have anything he could afford to risk, either. That handkerchief knot was real tight. Sam guessed he wanted to make some money bad, and he thought it a sorry thing for a country man to think he could make money that way.

Another fellow drifted up and waited while Good-Rocking Poppa, like a man uprooting thistle bushes, smoothed out the blanket with his feet. This new one was real drifty. His face turned three-four shades of light gray while Sam looked at him, and he didn't seem to have any eyes. If it hadn't been for his slick red shirt inside his city suit, Sam felt he might not have seen him at all. Between those two, Shorty was going to get chopped even shorter, for sure.

"Anybody else?" Poppa asked, all scorn. Nobody stirred. But when the three gambling men humped down to their knees to start their game, the rest of the passengers slid up on their haunches to watch better. They let Shorty have first shot with the dice. He was nervous, but was trying hard not to let his nerves show. "What with this train," he said, "this is sure a painless game. Just hold out your hand and that old locomotive will do your rolling for you. Except I don't want no boxcars, for sure."

"How much you betting?"

"Five and one-two-three. Eight cents. Start out small and win it all, a fellow told me. And he must have known what he said, because at Zac's Place — that's in Hattiesburg — he used to play by the hour, and he wasn't nothing but a turpentine-tapper like me, getting two dollars a day wages."

"Shoot, man, shoot."

Shorty shot. He didn't roll boxcars. He rolled snake-eyes. Poppa and the Spook sucked mocking wind through their teeth as they took away his coins, but Shorty didn't blink. "It's funny I had to come this far to meet these dice just when they was ready to do that," he mumbled, wondering-like. He peered at them in his hand like they were baby chicks he was trying to tell the sex of. "Think of all the times they been flung out. How come they couldn't have been flung just one more time before I got them? I bet a dime." He did better on the next roll — one point better. He made a three. The other two hissed even louder. "Don't take it too hard, son," Good-Rocking Poppa said. "All good hands start with craps." Shorty smiled like Poppa had really meant to wish him well, and he said, "These mules done run off with me so far that I don't know which would be the most trouble — to let 'em go and walk back, or try to get 'em to carry me home. Since I still got a hand on the reins, I guess I'll ride. Twenty cents."

He was green as grass, that Shorty. He put his pennies down on that blanket with sweetness and trust, like it was a church collection box. The amount he fished up left his handkerchief purse flat. Poppa drew in deep on his cigar and blew big-shot smoke. The Spook sat curled up on his spine like a snake. Shorty shoveled out the dice and spaded up the same one and two he had caught before. He kept his smile, but he wasn't able to talk. He dabbed at his nose with his empty handkerchief. Sam didn't like to see that kind of thing happen to a man.

"Or-or-or," old Poppa laughed. "Out of ammunition? Well, maybe we can talk some about bartering when the cash gets low all around. You," he asked the Spook, "you going to take up the hammer?" The Spook laid out a couple of dollar bills and the coins he had won from Shorty and took the dice.

Poppa matched his money. Then the Spook half stood up and began to take a bath with the dice. He rubbed them under his arms, behind his neck, even between his legs before he twisted around and let them go with his back turned to them. He made a seven. It was good for Good-Rocking Poppa that the Spook made a seven, Sam said to himself. He didn't like for a country man to be cheated, and he hadn't believed until then that those dice could roll a seven. If it hadn't turned out to be so, Poppa would have given Shorty his money back. At an ordinary time this would have seemed none of Sam's business, but leaving home and being alone makes a man draw up in himself all ready to pop like a spring.

"Well, well, the licorice whip hit a lick," Poppa joshed. "How much you bet now?" "Let it ride," the Spook whispered. Poppa stopped smiling, but shoveled bills out quick enough. The Spook wound up and delivered another seven. He rippled with inside laughter then whispered lower than before: "I bet it all." Poppa puffed, and with a mean motion had to dig in his pocket for money to cover the bet. He slapped down greenbacks, one by one, like a man who's not going to put up with this for long.

The Spook did his stuff with the dice, even more fancy than before, but pooped out a nine. His face went the color of a catfish's belly, and as he tried to make the point everything went into slow, like a movie-picture stunt Sam saw one time of a man diving into a tank of water. "Come on, man, get with it or get off it." Good-Rocking Poppa pushed him, but he rushed not a jot. Twist, bend, quiver, push — but all he rolled was five, three, ten, six. Old percentage had him and he was sweating. He rolled, but this time, most astonishing. one of the dice tripped on his finger and flew out through the open boxcar door. Gone.

Poppa jumped up. "Aheh! Aheh!" he blew through his

nose. The Spook made for to take his money back, but Poppa stomped at his hand. "It slipped. But I didn't lose," the Spook squeaked. "I want my money. I didn't lose."

"It slipped, hah? Well, go fetch that dice! Go fetch it! I'll guard the money till you come back. Hah, yes, I'll keep while you fetch. Fetch!" Poppa pounced and caught the collar of the Spook's nice red shirt. He pulled him down flat on his back and was dragging him for the door, however much the Spook twisted and grabbed.

He had him to the edge when a fellow in dungarees jumped up and said, "Stop that foolishment. I don't want to go to jail for none of your penny-nickel monkeyshines." This man didn't say it loud, but the scuffle stopped because it wasn't a man, but a woman in dungarees. What with the nighttime darkness, nobody had noticed before. She was pretty; hard but pretty. Her face was little darker than a peach, her hair lay flat and shiny black, with bangs across her forehead. She didn't yield to any man, Sam knew, the way her lean cheekbones and jaw stuck out to make an anvil for her slant eyes to flash on. And now he knew she was a woman, the points of her body stuck out against the blue rough clothes real ripe and ready. Everyone gazed like bird dogs around a bitch in springtime. The Spook slipped loose but didn't move far; he just sat and watched, too.

Poppa caught his wits the quickest. "Why sure, ma'am," he said smooth. "I guess this man accidental threw away that dice, after all. Take your money back," he purred to the Spook. "Just what you put up *at first,* that is. And leave down a dollar to pay me for that lost dice."

Sam didn't like Poppa's tipping his big white hat and hitching at his pants high and mighty. "If there is money being given back," he said, "then he should get his back, too." Sam pointed to Shorty, and Shorty looked up with Christmas eyes. Poppa popped air through his lips. He disliked this pushing in when he was trying to make up to the Woman, but he couldn't tell right off how tough Sam was.

The Woman looked at Sam, too, and he felt fire start inside. But he didn't think she could like him; he turned his thoughts to getting set for a fight for his fellow countryman's interests. Then the Woman said, "I think the little guy ought to have his dough," and Poppa had to give in. He made it clear it was a favor to her and used it as excuse to pass his hand across her back. Sam wanted to hit him, then thought that would be foolish and watched instead while Shorty put his nickels and pennies back in his handkerchief.

But Poppa's hot pants wouldn't allow peace to last. He scraped about, spreading his coat on the floor to make a seat for the Woman. She smiled and sat. He strutted in front of her, and with a hocus-pocus motion started rolling up one of his pants legs slow. Sam couldn't help staring, nor could the rest. He had a big black whiskey bottle stuck against his leg with adhesive tape. He snickered and pointed for her to undo it. She took one strip and pried it loose from his fat flesh real easy until she got near the end and then she popped it off with a snap. "Damn!" Poppa yelled and flapped up and down. The other passengers laughed and jeered. He started to cloud, but the Woman smiled up at him and said sweet, "It was stuck." He let her work at the other strip and just bit hard on his cigar when she popped him again.

When he sat close beside her and uncorked the bottle, it was too much for any man to stand. The raw teasing smell of that booze pulled Sam's nose until his stomach stretched and shivered. And when he looked to the bottle he saw Good-Rocking Poppa slobbering to lay hands on the Woman.

A fellow who had stayed quiet in the back until then jumped up and started a speech. He couldn't stand it any longer, either, Sam could see, and even before Sam measured him, if he had said "Let's throw that fat bastard off the train," Sam would have helped him do it. But he was a very young man, a pious man with some schooling, his words showed. This Teacher-Man said, "It is not right we should divide up like this. We are all going the same direction and sharing the same danger. Let's amuse each other with stories and fellowship. With a friendly drink or two, we could make a good party." This was mighty weak argument. Teacher-Man, tall and skinny, with two kinky shingles of hair balanced on his head, looked foolish in his prayer-meeting clothes, smiling a big horse-tooth smile.

The other men all nodded and backed him up, though, hoping against hope old Poppa would take the bait. He did not. "I appreciate your sentiments," he said syrup-smooth, "but I ain't got but this small fifth not even full. It wouldn't even start a party, and if I passed it around nobody would have sup enough to do them good. Besides, I'm faced with a situation that calls for stimulants." He clamped a hand on the Woman's thigh to show off what he meant by his last remark. Sam studied her to see what she might be thinking of this, but she had had some mileage, her, and the little lines that give away thoughts had rubbed off some time since.

"You all want to have a party?" Shorty spoke up. He could have been pushed off the train himself for being so stupid if he had not toddled over to a cardboard box that held his goods and come back with a gallon fruit jar that sparkled with the prettiest brown moonshine Sam ever saw. He set it down like a birthday cake, saying, "My uncle gave me this for to offer any policeman who might catch me." Shorty sure surprised Sam. He was going to sit there with his jailhouse insurance tucked away and going thirsty, no matter how much Good-Rocking Poppa taunted; but when he finally understood that others were yearning bad, he offered his jar up. He was a country man, all right.

Everybody gathered, squatting to each side of Poppa and the Woman. Poppa held his bottle close to him and grumbled: "I bet that stuff strikes them blind." But he was shamed and his rooster wings were trimmed. "We going to tell stories?" Shorty asked when he handed the jar to Teacher-Man to start off the drinking. Teacher-Man looked blank, but had the wit to take a swig before looking blank again. Nobody had meant to tell stories. That was only talk for pushing Poppa.

"Didn't they teach you in school, ladies first?" the Woman asked of Teacher-Man, making him jump and slosh the whiskey in rushing it to her. She took a man-size swallow and a second; Sam knew she had asked for the fruit jar, instead of taking from Poppa's black bottle, in order to show where her sympathy was. But when she passed the jar to Sam, and he wasn't the next one to her, he didn't know what she meant. She said then, "Now how about some happy stories to kill the hours?"

"Why sure," Teacher-Man agreed. He scratched his head. "Why don't we each in turn tell all about ourselves?" That was a bad idea. Nobody wanted to meet head-on with their pasts; everybody was running from it. The party fell so quiet that the only sound was of the whiskey trickling down a man's throat and splashing on his bottom rib. They scrunched uncertain and uncomfortable, like ants on the land, until the Woman said, "I'd rather hear stories about white people. There's a lot of interesting things about white people." She giggled deep and mean. Before Sam could separate one white man he knew and not confuse him with the others, Good-Rocking Poppa had took over. "I got a lively story to tell," he said. And after he had fiddled with lighting his cigar he told his story.

Good-Rocking Poppa's Story

THERE WAS a doctor in New Orleans who was better than most. He had a big office in a glass building downtown, and even if Negro people had to wait in the drugstore across the street, you got your true turn in line and didn't have to wait too long. The extra trip to go to the office to tell the nurse and then out to the store and then back when she called was bad, but this doctor specialized in belly pains and didn't get too many with broken legs. His name was Dr. Morris. I went to him to get the whiskey holes in my belly patched.

One day he stopped in the middle of joshing me about eating too many pork chops, the way he usually did when he wrote out a chit for medicine, and said, "I wonder could you tell me a place where I might take some friends for a good time." I thought he meant a whorehouse and was thinking what to say. He saw I thought he meant a whorehouse and colored up. He was pink-face naturally, a round man who had awful thin hair for as young as he looked. Maybe medical college does that to them. He looked like a straight-and-narrow man, too, but looks don't mean character. I would have told him a good place to get a lay, except he said, "I mean a night club where we can see some *real* colored entertainers. These friends of mine are coming from Connecticut and I don't want to take them to the run-of-the-mill French Quarter tourist trap. I'd like to show them the real thing; you know, where the floor show is legitimate."

Now sending a white man to a cat-house is one thing, but a night club is another. There's too much drinking and big talk in most clubs, and I could not see my advantage if the doctor got himself sliced up and rolled on my advice. But still, whatever this favor might take off his bill to me would be appreciated, so I thought and told him, "Dr. Morris, I think your friends might like the Elite Treat Club at 123½ Dryades. Be sure to tell the man at the door I said for you to come."

When he heard me say that last, he smiled like he figured I was hinting about the doctor bill, which was all right, but he was wrong. The Elite Treat is just the opposite of the old saying; it is "for damn few niggers and no whites." Was he not to use my name at the door — because I had a certain standing in the community — he and his Yankee friends was doomed to see the street. Of course, after they got in, they would have to sit back where the waiters stacked their trays and behind a stout mahogany pillar, while out on the ice-blue dance floor black couples glided around, their fancy clothes — tuxes and long dresses, no jitterbug stuff — reflected back by the purple-glass ceiling. Those that wouldn't be dancing would be sitting at tables with white linen cloths, talking across to their friends by the gold light of old-fashion street lamps that burned real candles. The waiters there were dressed like cavalry horses and acted twice as high and mighty. But I didn't worry about the snubbing Dr. Morris and his friends would get, I thought it would be educational.

There is a lot of money among some New Orleans Negroes, but it has no place to go. That is why, even though it is situated over a grocery store, the Elite Treat is the duplicate of the hoity-toity club in the city's biggest lily-white hotel, they tell me. It gives those black people which can afford to a chance to prove themselves. For entertainment, though, the white hotel couldn't copy the Elite Treat. Nothing but the best. And the best of the best was Lula Blue. She could sing to make a one-eyed man go blind. She was a big girl with copper skin and she wore her hair high with streaks of red, like fire was in it. She sang like she liked a good time, and she did, for true.

Dr. Morris and his friends went to the Elite Treat and seemed to enjoy themselves, I heard. And later I heard that Dr. Morris came back by himself. Not once, but two-three times. When I went to his office for treatment he said, "My friends liked the Elite Treat," and nothing else. But he kept on going back. In due time I found out it wasn't for the five-dollar chicken dinner; he was courting Lula Blue.

I don't have to tell you what a serious thing it is for a Negro girl to step across the line, especially of her free will, going out of her way to. Lula Blue could have had a hospital full of Negro doctors, if it was money or free medical advice she wanted. She went out of her way, all right.

One night I went to the House of Uncle Charley to see if a card game was going. Uncle Charley's is a little shack where longshoremen hang out. It isn't much, not even a sign in front, only a blackboard to mark up what docks are going to need loading gangs. Inside, there is a counter at which Charley sells poor-boy sandwiches and beer, a juke box, some tables, and a back booth for "ladies." It is a good place to gamble, though. When those longshoremen work they make real money and like to spend it. Charley plays a mean hand himself and keeps things quiet so a man can concentrate on his cards. He turns the juke box off at seven at night, and he doesn't allow the street girls to hang around and noise up the place with their yackety-yack. They can look in, but if there ain't no stray men they pass on by. If they see a man they can come in and state their price, and whether he says yes or no they go right out. No bargaining, no bumming drinks, that's Charley's rules.

That night Charley and the regulars were hunched up at the counter, talking about something foolish like politics, while behind them the card table sat lonesome. "What's all this, everybody broke?" I asked. "Or did the landlord die?" Charley's trick eye flickered left and right like a stop signal, and his good eye wasn't too happy either. He opened one hand to show me a crispy green twenty-dollar bill then closed it again, leaving his first finger sticking out and pointing at the wall of the "ladies booth." Without another word I walked over to fiddle with the juke box — it was hooting away later than it was supposed to — in order to get a look inside the booth. There they were, drinking beer and talking like two canaries: Dr. Morris and Lula Blue.

Old Charley had his worries, all right. He didn't have enough influence to keep his tail out of the crack if somebody who had hard feeling against him should see this and go tell the precinct sergeant. If the two had been on the floor screwing it would have been better — but black and white talking! Charley was earning the double sawbuck the Doctor paid him to let them in. I thought I had the right to hear what I could, so I sat down on the end stool nearest the booth and let my eyes count the flies on a loaf of French bread behind the counter while my ears stretched out.

He was saying: "I didn't ever want to be a doctor very bad. Only when I started making enough money to buy things and do things to take my mind off my practice, that's when I could say I enjoyed my practice. But now I've bought all the things and done all the things a man can for himself, and I feel stuffed and half dead. Or that is, I felt stuffed until . . . "

She said, "You do things every day for people. You make them get well and feel good. You have to think on that. Of course I understand your worry. I stand up in front of the hot lights and make a fool of myself for a bunch of drunks, and the surest way to ease my mind is to count the clothes and jewels I own. It is hard to believe that you are doing good by giving those people something to lose their work-day blues."

He said, "You can't tell yourself that yourself. You have to have somebody you respect — and love — beside you . . . "

She said, "You got to have guts to eat a sandwich. You got to have guts to do anything. Nobody can lend you their guts."

I didn't understand all that they were talking about, but I know enough of people's voice tones to tell that he was chasing after her and she was staying just out of reach. But Lula Blue shouldn't have let him bring her here where the two-bits-a-roll girls go. He being white could not know, but she should. I vowed to go see her the next morning and give her a fatherly talk.

Next morning I didn't see her. I went to Miss Lizzie's, where Lula Blue had a room. Miss Lizzie told me she was gone, and how she told me made me know she had told her to go. For the first time I knew that this doctor affair wasn't just a freak, it was big trouble. There stood Miss Lizzie, and I'd bet that two hundred pounds of her three hundred pounds was Italian, and in those Working Girl rooms she rented in that brown wooden house between a barroom and a filling station I'd bet that more than a few were resting up after working under a white man all night. But she stood there like God's bitch watchdog.

A couple days later I learned Lula Blue was staying at the Hay Market. This isn't the true name of the hotel, but it is always called that because country people moving to the city generally stay there. The room she had smelled like an outdoor toilet, and her fine clothes and gee-gaws looked sad, draped over the skinned-up furnishings for lack of closets. When I pushed aside enough stuff to let me sit on a wicker chair, I was almost afraid to put my feet on the dirty bamboo rug for fear it would rub off something. But Lula Blue was not noticing where she lived.

"Have you gone back to reefers again?" I asked sarcastic.

"The kind of fire that has me high don't make no smoke," she said pleased-like, rubbing her hand over the bosom of her blue nylon kimono.

"Strikes me you must have slept with a white man some time before."

"Sure. But it was just because he was white. I slept with lots of men before, but always for one reason or another, not for the man himself."

"You're talking like a schoolgirl."

"I feel like a schoolgirl."

"Well, look, girl, I took the trouble to come to this crummy hotel to warn you to act your age. You know this city don't have patience for the kind of game you're playing. You have a good job and some social standing; you're going to lose it all if you keep on this way."

She lay on her back on the squeaky bed and smiled at the ceiling. "I'm in too deep to pull chips now. And the odds is always big on anything good. I don't think losing could be worse than not taking a chance."

I flipped my hat brim and left, and didn't concern myself more until the Elite Treat fired Lula Blue. They told her it was because they planned a new-style floor show, but there was no doubt why. They didn't want no scandal. At that, I tucked my courage in my hands and vowed to face Dr. Morris with the facts. But a Negro man has no words that a white man can understand besides "Yessir." I didn't do no good.

"Dr. Morris," I spoke up, "your business is your business, especially your private business. But I couldn't help hearing things in my neighborhood that might mean trouble for you and another party."

"I could have guessed. I could have expected it," he spit out scornful, his pink face puckered sour and his hand shaky among his tools. "How much do you want?" He thought I was looking for blackmail money. I was a second realizing this, and another second passed before I decided that maybe blackmail would scare him away from Lula Blue. I said, "Twenty dollars for now. But us blackmailers ain't never satisfied. The more we learn the more we want."

"Now look, you!" Dr. Morris said while he took out his wallet and threw me a bill. "I don't care what I have to pay you hyenas; I don't know any price you can put on a real true thing." Despite what he said I walked out thinking maybe I had put the fear of God in him.

But those two carried on like before. I learned that he had rented for her a little house in Back-A-Town, where nobody asks questions much. I saw her driving one of those open-top foreign-make cars, wearing a black satin sweater with a little dog sitting by her. There couldn't anything look cozier.

Then one day she came to my room when I was between life and death because of a long night with the bottle. She fidgeted and finally asked me if I would look around for a singing job for her. "Not because anything's wrong," she said. "And I don't need the money. I just feel the need to pass a little time."

The hangover made me quick to pay her out. But I had more reasons, too. My part in leading to what she had done wasn't secret and didn't help my standing none. "You couldn't get work flushing toilets in the men's room," I told her. "You nowhere. Everybody feels you scoffed at them by crossing the line; you can't come back across because they don't want to scoff at you — you'd make them sick-mad to look at. You nowhere."

She didn't spit fire like the old Lula Blue would have, but sort of wilted and drifted out.

Right after that she and Dr. Morris, both stinking drunk and shouting at themselves, were denied entrance to the Elite Treat. Then things got desperate. She took to waiting for him outside his office, in broad daylight, to drive him home. On Sundays she made him ride her through City Park, where no Negroes is ever allowed. Lula Blue had lost her own perch and like a bird beating against a plate-glass window was trying to get inside his world. This was a shoe on the other foot, and I wondered how Dr. Morris liked the pinch.

The worst thing happened not long later, but it was so funny I would have given sixty dollars to see it. She and him went to the International House for cocktails. The International House stands like a big slice of cheese in the heart of town and is the meeting place for muckety-mucks from everywhere, all over the world. They don't even hire Negro help for fear it might unease some coffee-color South America president. But Lula Blue went. She didn't go as herself, of course. She put on three-four strings of pearls and made a dress out of a window drape. Best of all, she glued a fat rhinestone in the middle of her forehead — she was an Indian princess from far-off Asia! Man, she gave those folks a time of it. They told me she bollixed up the language so bad they couldn't understand what she ordered and had them apologizing when they brought the wrong thing. She even made them fetch her a highball of goat's milk and bonded whiskey, with a cherry on top.

She fooled everybody — except herself and, I bet, the Doctors' Association. They must have added two and two together and put the screws on Dr. Morris. He and Lula Blue didn't gallivant around any more from then on; they stuck inside that Back-A-Town house like two prisoners. I didn't see her again — not for sure, that is. Once at Uncle

Charley's I looked up from my hole card and through the grease on the front glass I thought I saw her face peering in, but it was such a ghosty glimpse, and was gone so quick, that I didn't go out to check.

Only horseplayers read the white newspapers in New Orleans, and me, I learned long time ago that betting horses is foolishment; I save my eyes for better things than the squeentsy print of entries and results. But one day a horseplayer drew a ring around a little story in the paper and passed the sheet to me. NEGRESS SINGER FOUND DEAD, the headline said. Lula Blue had broke her neck down a flight of stairs in that Back-A-Town house and the police thought it an accident. She was by herself at the time, it said. The man at the morgue told me she had been three-four months gone with child.

I went to Dr. Morris' office and didn't leave the nurse's desk until he came out and led me into his inner room. He acted like he expected me. He said, "It went all wrong. I didn't think anything so good could go that wrong. If you want to shoot, point the gun out the window. Shoot them while they stand there waiting for the stoplight to change and you won't miss a single law-abiding, God-fearing, God-damned one of them. They are the ones you should shoot."

His words was too complicated for me to follow at that moment, and I feared that if I stopped to think, I wouldn't do what I came to do. All I felt was that if a rich white man can kill a black girl, then a poor black man can kill a white, for if he can't, then no black man is a man. I shot.

Of course, I proved my point to only one of all the white folks that it needs proving to, and he's dead — so in that respect, what I did was a foolish thing. Like I said, he acted like he expected me, probably because Lula Blue had told him I was her brother. But I don't think the bastard expected me to shoot.

Good-Rocking Poppa's story left the boxcar riders big-eyed with feeling. Sam, though, didn't believe a man of the kind Poppa seemed to be could do a deed such as he described. He picked at the truth of the story a little: "If I had the money that doctor had, I'd moved to someplace where I could've been left with Lula Blue in peace."

Nobody backed up his remark. Instead, the Woman snapped scorn at him: "Where is that place?"

"I think their spirit broke someplace along the middle of things and they just hung together not thinking about ways to escape; they just hung together, doomed," Teacher-Man said. And what he said sounded right to Sam, but Sam could not make himself think the more of Good-Rocking Poppa. He had to admit to himself that he was jealous of him because of the Woman.

"That's true," Shorty chimed in. "When people's spirit is broke they won't even get off their haunches and come inside if it's raining hot stove lids. Why, back in Silcox County the poor people there — "

The Woman interrupted him. "I don't want to hear no more sad stories. If you're going to tell a story, it'd better be a happy story."

"This is got a happy part, but it ain't about a white person, though. It's about a dog. Did you ever hear about the Talking Dog?" Shorty asked. Everybody shook their heads, and Shorty started off on his story.

Shorty's Story

LIKE I SAID, the poor people of Silcox County was mighty low in spirit. Between three rich white families and the Dixie Pride Lumber Company there wasn't an acre's ground or a nickel change lying loose. You had to hoe cotton on shares or chop pine for twenty-five cents an hour in the Compound. They called the Dixie Pride establishment the Compound because after renting one of the company houses and buying at the company store, when payday came you didn't have money enough to do more than get into the company picture show on credit.

The cotton land was playing out, and more and more folks had to go to the Compound. But at the Compound the electric saw and power log stacker weeded out workers left and right. Only the turpentine-tappers worked steady, and there was talk of paying them by the resin bucket instead of the hour, while at the same time docking their wages if they drained too much from one tree.

Then they heard the Talking Dog had come to Silcox County. Folks said he had been run out of Alabama for trying to organize a union in the sawmill in Washington County. And before that, he used to watch the basket-counters down in the orange fields at Groveland, Florida, until the Ku Kluxers got on him. But despite all that hard-luck trail, the people was glad he had come to their county, because he was a wondrous thing.

He didn't look like much. He come trotting down the dusty road, his tail stiff-out for traveling—an ordinary pointer bird dog, you'd think, not near pretty enough to be a picture on a tobacco can. He had a liver-color patch over one eye and down an ear, like a pirate or clown. His hide was ghost-white except for a sprinkling of black dots. He snurfed left and right, his head low, as he went along. When he met a man he looked him up and down, shifted his whiskery chops around, and kept on moving. But he did a heap of good, that old Talking Dog. Early in the morning he'd gather up the little children and march them off to school, patrolling around them circlewise so none would slip off into the woods. When they got inside, those scapers wouldn't raise their noses from their books for fear he might be looking in. After that chore the Talking Dog would cut back and pay his morning visit to the settlements. At one place he'd stop a woman from putting too much salt in the stew, and at another the gossiping would cease and the clotheswashing commence when he passed by. He protected the chastity of a couple of homes, too, by staring Back-Door Johnnies down. And Blind Tom, eighty-nine and sitting on the porch to meet death halfway, would laugh like a stallion when they told him the Talking Dog had come a-calling.

About noon, if the sun was bright, he'd stretch out in the shade wherever he might be and slice off a nap, laying flat almost, on his back, with his hind legs spread and his sex organ bolder than brass. He was a sight! Then around two o'clock he'd haul himself up, flap his ears against the side of his head to get the dust out, and start overseeing the men at work. He'd go along the rows, spying where the weeds hadn't been chopped close enough to the cotton stalk or lending a hand to get an old mule moving. Out in the Dixie Pride woods the Talking Dog pointed out squirrels and wild grape patches for a man to take home for supper, and if a man wanted to rest and chew the fat, he'd mosey along the resin cups and see that they didn't spill. Or if they wasn't filling up so good, he'd pee-pee in them to get the job done faster.

Now the Talking Dog didn't talk much, that wasn't his way. He was what the white politicians call a confidential adviser, sort of. If he saw anybody needed a word of warning, he'd beckon the person aside and tell him private, and make him promise not to let anybody know where he got the word. Naturally, all the people wanted to be close by should there be any advice passed out, and they liked the idea of having the Talking Dog on watch outside their house at night in case the sheriff or some pool-room rowdies would come to do some window shooting, so he had a pan of good grits and gravy waiting for him in back of every shack. A turpentine-tapper named Joe Dabbs was sure honored when the Talking Dog made his house his headquarters.

I said there wasn't but two ways to make a nickel in Silcox, chopping cotton or chopping wood, but there was a third, too. Sheriff Johnson had a great scheme to aid the Negro people of his county. He and his deputies would bless a man every Monday with three sacks of sugar and tell him they expected fifteen gallons of moonshine by Friday. On Friday they collected the fifteen gallons and divided it among three other Negro men and told them they wanted thirty dollars Monday. Those three men had to hustle out over their neighborhoods and spread the good cheer among the thirsty weekend ramblers. Nobody volunteered for this proposition; a dime a gallon was all both maker and seller got, but you had to make the quota, rain or shine, if out of your own pocket. The sheriff selected who he favored and it wasn't thought wise to trifle with the favor.

Now Joe Dabbs was a seller and so the Talking Dog came to learn what was going on. He saw that cloudy mean stuff being dropped at the door in dirty vinegar jugs. He saw Joe have to leave his wife and children and take up his burden among the places of sinful pleasure. He poked his nose inside the Blue Flame and the Dew Drop Inn while Joe was trying to sell his goods. You couldn't tell what he made of it all, but he was studying. He saw the raw rotgut turn decent men into killers and innocent girls into whores.

One Saturday night a pitiful thing happened in the Blue Flame. A respected barber by name of Adam Brown got so drunk he did not know who he was, and stabbed his fourteen-year-old daughter because she would not let him put his hand up her dress. She had come there to fetch him home. I think it was this that led the Talking Dog to unfold his plan.

The next Monday Deputy Battle went around in his pickup truck, delivering sugar for the new batch of moonshine to be cooked with. But nobody ran out to unload their share.

"I'm sorry, Deputy Battle, sir," one man said when he stopped at his place, "but I'm in the midst of becoming sanctified and I'm pledged to quit shining for a spell."

"I'm sorry, Deputy Battle, sir, but I'm scared. My wife Sarah is sure she saw a government man sneaking around back last night. How'd she know it was a government man? He had a big white hat on and didn't leave any tracks where he walked, that's how. I'm too scared."

"I'm sorry, Deputy Battle, sir, but my old venerable disease is giving me such misery I can't squat long enough to kindle the fire under the still."

Each place he went, old Battle found some sort of trouble, and after he had made his last visit he still had as many sacks as when he started. He turned around to speed back to the sheriff's office to tell what he had experienced, but somehow some of the sugar sifted into the gas tank of his truck and he finished his journey on a borrowed mule.

At this same time Deputy Wilson had gone out in the official car to collect money from the sellers. He tooted the big horn. Out came a seller with three full jugs. "What you got there, boy?" Deputy Wilson asked, surprised. "I couldn't sell these nohow, Deputy Wilson, sir." Now Deputy Wilson wasn't too smart a man and this had never happened before. He chucked his double chin and scratched his bald head under his hat and decided he had better take the whiskey back. With three jugs on the seat by him he rolled down the road a piece and tooted again. He got for his pains a little money and some more full jugs. Each stop he made it was the same, and the car was bulging with jugs. Some of them's corks wasn't on too tight, neither. They smelled him coming when he was two miles out of town. And when Deputy Battle drew near town, an hour later, they heard him *three* miles out, persuading that sorry mule.

Sheriff Johnson listened through his men's tale of grief. He leaned back in his leather chair and undid the wide gunbelt that kept his belly pinched in small. He was a suspicious man, but he decided to wait, in case this really was just a happenstance bad week. The Negro people of Silcox County could give some thanks that he was operating the bootleg business. He couldn't shoot them all, because then he wouldn't have no customers.

Friday came, but no moonshine was delivered to the sellers. Nobody suffered much from thirst, though; people was staying close to home, wondering how this was going to turn out and thinking sober thoughts. On Monday Deputy Battle and Deputy Wilson drove out together to hand out the sugar to the makers. But everywhere they got excuses, no matter how they clouded up and patted their guns. They drove off cussing to tell the sheriff. All the people knew the sheriff would do some devilment now, and more than one or two might have hitched up and gone with their hat in their hand to beg their sugar if the Talking Dog hadn't been moving around the community, taking the measure of every man.

Sheriff Johnson had heard about the Talking Dog; every white person in the county had, one way or another. They figured it was a lot of darky foolishment. Except Sheriff Johnson was shrewd. He reasoned there was some connection with the moonshine trouble, and since it was said the Talking Dog stayed at Joe Dabbs' house, he decided Joe was the leader of the trouble.

Joe Dabbs was weeding collard greens in his little garden when the sheriff's long car slunk up the road. At that moment he had no place to go but under his house. Only his wife and the Talking Dog was left to greet the sheriff when he strutted into the yard, his shiny cowboy boots cutting chunks out of the earth. Although he was tall and weighed more than two hundred pounds, his head was little and pinched up, making it hard to separate his features. The only way you could tell how he felt was to measure the redness of his face and neck. His face showed real red now under his wide-brim white hat and his fat hand sat heavy on the pearl-handle gun at his hip. With that gunbelt pushing his stomach up into his chest he looked for all the world like a mean fighting rooster. "Where's Joe?" he asked, steel-sharp.

Mrs. Dabbs was not a small woman, herself. She stood taller than most men, and was smooth all over with solid muscle. Not that she wasn't womanly in the right places, no indeed; her bosoms were big and firm and rose up to a point that made you squirm, and she had a slow soft smile. But now fear and anger stirred her, and her eyes froze to the ground. She kept squeezing on the handle of the hoe she had been helping Joe with. "I don't know," she whispered.

"Come on, woman, tell me where's Joe."

"I don't know."

Sheriff Johnson got redder than fresh blood. He moved forward like he wanted to hit her, but the hoe stopped him. Instead he drew his pistol. "Woman, I give you five seconds to tell me where your husband is." Mrs. Dabbs just raised her eyes to his and glared.

But Joe under the house couldn't stand it no longer and was starting to climb out when the Talking Dog was waked up by the fuss. He had been catching his noontime sleep. He put one foot at a time to the ground and shook out his ears. Then like an old man who needs glasses he squinched his eyes up and down until he recognized the sheriff. "Waroof!" he bellowed in a tone that rattled the piney wood. And he stood there with his tail quivering and his nose pointing Sheriff Johnson the way to Hell.

The sheriff hadn't noticed him before and jumped at the sound of his voice. He looked and realized who he was. "So this is the Talking Dog," he sneered. "This is the high muckety-muck of a voodoo animal that's causing trouble. Well, Talking Dog, I want to hear you talk. I'm going to give *you* five seconds to tell me where Joe Dabbs is." And he turned the gun on him.

The Talking Dog didn't say a word. He didn't even blink, but stood there like a brave gunfighter in a Saturday night movie, daring Sheriff Johnson to do his damnedest. He didn't say a word when the sheriff shot, but just fell down and died with his head on his arm.

That shot brought all the neighbor folks a-running. When they saw the Talking Dog dead and the sheriff with a smoking pistol, they bunched together and made a fist of people in their anger. The sheriff saw them and decided not to shoot Mrs. Dabbs. In fact, he decided to get back in his long car and round up a posse from town before he took up looking for Joe Dabbs again.

I think the Talking Dog had figured that the shot would bring the people to save Mrs. Dabbs and Joe. I think he was tired of wandering the dusty roads, bringing the word to the Negroes of the South. He must have figured all the sides of the matter and decided that a sheriff's bullet is an honorable way to die.

There was some who hoped for magic and that he would come to life, but the Talking Dog was dead, for true. They buried him under a pine cross.

That same night, though, Joe Dabbs' bitch bird dog had six pups, all boys, with liver patches over one eye, ghost-white with black dots.

When Shorty had finished, the Spook asked, "This we're drinking ain't none of the sheriff's coffin liner, is it?"

"No sir, this is real-corn personal stock," Shorty said with a smile, but his eyes were far-off sad.

Teacher-Man butted in real big: "That is the trouble with too many of our people. They lie to themselves and make up things. They lean on superstition instead of facing the hard road to salvation. Our people think the God of Right is for white folks and that they can hide in the darkness and worship sinful idols . . ."

"What you talking about, man? This fellow tells a funny story about a dog and you start spitting thunderbolts," Good-Rocking Poppa complained, and Sam agreed with him. Then he figured that Teacher-Man was not used to drinking nothing much stronger than communion grape juice, and he is not criticizing Shorty, it is his whiskey talking.

Whatever it was, both of Teacher-Man's arms jerked up

and down, jostling the kinky planks of hair on his head, and he seemed to scrape his words off his big teeth with his lips. He talked on about the Blessed Redeemer who allowed himself to be crucified to save a place in Heaven for all those persons who follow the True Faith, be they rich or poor or black or white. Sam didn't listen too close because he had heard the words many times before but never had seen no proof of them. He was willing to let the man talk on, if he felt strong about the subject, and besides, a pious thought or two couldn't hurt in this harsh situation.

Sam let his eyes glide along the country outside. They were rolling through Alabama now. It seemed the land was getting more humps in it, but maybe that was because, until not too long ago, Sam thought to go up North you had to go uphill all the way. That idea came from the times he looked at the map on the school house wall and saw that the North was up at the top.

But one thing sure, this train wouldn't have chugged this slow if it was rolling from north to south. It kept a man stewing a long time over the same coals — Alabama was just like Mississippi, Sam had heard, and Birmingham was ahead, crawling with hard-fisted policemen. Still, even if it was slow enough to make a man think he was drowning, it made ripples that tickled the mind. Maybe, maybe, maybe, the wheels kept saying over and again.

And a Maybe drew his glance to the Woman, who was sitting looking bored and pushing Good-Rocking Poppa's head off her shoulder. He was pretending to be asleep. Her eyes met Sam's eyes and she gave him a smile with one side of her face. But a Maybe and a real woman are two different things, and his native caution rose. He had but twenty-two dollars to supply him on his way; he could not afford a fancy woman. As if she had read his thoughts, her smile turned to a frown of scorn. She jerked her head away and said sharp to Teacher-Man: "I think you preached enough. If you're going to talk some more, then tell a story. That's the rules."

Teacher-Man stopped his bobbing and psalm-saying right off. "You're right, ma'am. Nothing can prove truths like a good story."

Teacher-Man's Story

A FELLOW name of George Little lived in a town I won't name. It was a small town built around the courthouse square. On one side of the square stood the Baptist church of brick, at the opposite end, the Methodist church with a yellow stucco front. Along both of the other sides sat the stores, looking all alike behind their tin-roof awnings. The courthouse, orange brick, was almost buried in shrubs; only its greenish copper dome stuck out clear. Morning or afternoon, when it didn't rain, the livest spot in town was the domino game on the concrete table under the live-oak tree just behind the concrete statue of Our Confederate Hero.

George Little worked for a laundry where his mother had got him a job instead of letting him finish the tenth grade at the high school. He rode a bicycle with a big basket on it, picking up bundles and delivering them. He had had this job for two-three years but never learned to like the stink of mussy linen or the heavy burden of starched clean clothes. He'd ride along the asphalt streets with his eyes shut against the sun, thinking how he could make up for the graduating certificate he didn't get, straining to see a way to better himself despite his lack.

His brooding caused him to be careless, and one day he

rode right into the back end of a truck, smashing the front wheel of the bike and spraining his ankle, too. But the hurt was piddling compared to the trouble he caught when he told the laundry owner what happened. The man would have fired George right then, except that his mother was the best shirt presser he had. So what he did was charge George with the damages and tell him to do his job on foot until a new wheel came from Sears, Roebuck.

This made a hard penalty. George had the choice of breaking his back by carrying a stack of bundles in his arms or wearing his legs out walking back and forth with one bundle at a time. But, like the good Lord decrees, the best of blessings sprout from dark hardship. It was in this way he was allowed to meet with Major Carling. Not that he hadn't seen the Major before, riding through town on his big gray horse, but George had always been on his bicycle at the same time and they had passed each other by, each on their own business, with George paying no mind even though a man on a horse was unusual downtown.

But one day when George was dragging one foot after the other across the road between the laundry and the square, suffering his heavy bundle, the gray horse moved up to in front of him and he nearly walked into it without seeing. When he stopped, surprised, a big red hand stuck a leaflet at him. He looked up into the face af Major Carling. Though the Major was a heavy man, his face was so heavy-jawed and long it looked lean, and though it was red, it was pale, too; a kind of frosted red, you could say, just like the shocks of hair poking out from his black hat were red with wintery white streaks mixed through. His eyes were bright red around the rims, but he seemed to have no lips beneath his long nose, just a straight line. He didn't say anything while he held the leaflet out for George to take.

No white man had ever given George anything much in

his life, especially reading matter. George thought of politicians' handbills. No politician ever gave a Negro man a handbill. A Negro man wouldn't take one neither, for fear the people around would believe he was planning to sign up to vote. But the horse blocked George's path, making him shift his bundle and accept.

When the Major trotted off, George started to drop the paper to the street in case the sheriff or anybody was watching from the courthouse window, but he happened to glimpse a drawing on it. In bold black strokes a flaming sword was pictured swooping down out of the sky and heading straight for a scared bunch of people, not one of them a bit as big as the sword. "Vengeance is Mine, said the Lord" was printed under that, and then, farther down: "I have a message for those who have the courage to hear. Respectfully, Andrew C. Carling." There was nothing else. George figured that this had to do with religion and he thought, in his blindness, that he knew about religion. He knew religion as big words and loud songs every Sunday, and Wednesday nights, too, for women. He had never seen a preacher who handled himself half as proper as Principal Ballard of the high school. But the idea of a sword striking down the people who pestered him took George's fancy, and because a white man had brought the idea it was mysterious and exciting. He stood watching the Major ride around the corner of the square and stop alongside the domino game. Although most of the six-seven men at the table were the Major's age and must have known him, nobody paid him heed. He sat still on his horse, holding his leaflets out like they was a deck of cards and he was seeking somebody to play.

George made a desperate decision. He hitched up his bundle and walked after the Major. When he stood by the horse he didn't know what to say. The Major didn't look down.

Finally George tapped the man's leg with the leaflet and asked, "Do you have a message for me, sir?" The Major peered at George with his red eyes, his face not showing anything, but his motion had the look of a fisherman whose day's work had landed him just a little perch. "Follow me," he said, and poked his horse.

The two of them, one riding, one walking, went around the square and turned off down the street that led to the best white folks' houses. George was having a hard time to keep up, what with his bundle, and too, he began to have fears. But when he thought of the bawling out the laundry man would have prepared for him now, he stayed near the Major. After two blocks he got so hot and bothered with all the things plaguing his body and his mind that he had to do something. So George said goodbye to the laundry by flinging his bundle into the ditch.

The houses on each side of them were back off the road, all old and white, dignified with tall pillars, sleepy with drawn shutters. George knew there was an eager eye behind every shutter, spying all that passed. They moved along until they came to the last house on the left. It was like the others, except the paint had about gone and weeds had taken over the yard. There was an old barn, too, where most of the other places had car garages. The Major stopped and pointed to the barn. "Creep through the field and get in the barn from the back door," he said. "My godless daughters might interfere."

George didn't want to be seen by the Major's daughters, neither, but he was surprised to hear Miss Emma and Miss Rachel called godless. He could never tell the two apart, they were both skinny and wore glasses and had frizzy hair. One worked in the courthouse and the other taught at the high school, he knew, and he wondered if godless people were allowed to work in such places. He remembered his mother laughing one time about how the Carling sisters would fuss at each other over the telephone, the one at the school shouting, "I know he's right out there on the square disgracing himself and us. Go down there and send him home!" And the one at the courthouse shouted back, "I've done it too often already. If you feel so strong about it, you come down and get him." The gossip hadn't meant anything to George at the time, but he guessed there was some family dispute. "Move, boy," the Major ordered, and George, putting aside his thoughts, said, "Yessir," and started sneaking to the barn, feeling pleasurable big, like a soldier in battle.

The barn wasn't much of a barn. It leaned to one side, the loft had rotted away and the floorboards were inch-deep with dried horse turds. Nobody ever seemed to clean the hay up neither, but just tossed layer on layer and let it rot and smell. Right after George had pushed his way in through the one-hinged back door the Major clattered in on the horse. He got off the horse, patted it on the throat, and without looking at George, said, "I'll be back after supper. Wait."

One of the Major's legs was stiff at the knee, and as he walked off, every other step made him bounce and sway to one side, like he was hitting the ground before he expected to. George noticed the saddle hadn't been taken off the horse or anything. The horse nudged him with its hip and looked him in the eye, so he decided the Major had left taking care of it to him. He fiddled around with the horse and the hay, wondering what words the Major would say after supper and if he would bring him a plate of food, too. As it started getting darker and later, he began thinking mostly about food. When he peeped out the barn and saw all the lights turned out at the house, he thought about slipping away to his home. He was too big now for his mama to beat, but he knew she would chew at him almost all night for what he'd done. He sat on the floor worrying, resting his back against the horse, which had squatted down to sleep. Then he saw it likely that the Major was testing him, that this was his initiation. He took heart, despite his empty stomach and the stinking barn, and fell off to sleep beside the horse.

Next morning early the Major punched George awake with his boot toe. "Who are you?" he asked, harsh and surprised. George twisted away from the boot hitting his ribs and rose to a crouch. "I'm George Little, sir," he answered. "What are you doing here?" the Major asked, and George knew from the tone that he was being accused of being a thief or something. He was madder than scared, though, in his puzzlement. "You said you had a message for me," he said, head down. The Major backed off, blinked his red eyes, then humped back and forth across the barn floor. He said at last, real low, "You came to hear my message?" George looked at the Major's face and saw that his thin mouth was twitching. It seemed nobody had ever asked for his message until then, and George felt pity for the man.

"You are a Christian?" the Major asked, his voice up big again. George said yes. "You are a sinner?" George said no. "You are a nigra, so you are a sinner," the Major said flat-out and George didn't say anything. "How can you be a Christian and a sinner at the same time? How can you?" the Major asked, and George didn't know.

"I am a sinner, but, praise God, I am a Christian, too!" The Major had his wind up. He slapped himself on the chest and looked up through the holes in the roof. "Because I am a sinner, I am a true Christian. I am as black as a nigra in sin, I stink with sin, but I will ride along the golden avenues to the wonderful mansion prepared for me. I will be saved because I am an open sinner. In the darkness of night, the blessed Scripture says, you shall see the stars. I see the stars.

But—" the Major grabbed George's shoulder so hard he tipped back on his haunches and would have fallen if the Major hadn't held him up by his shirt—"the secret sinners in the Ford cars, lusting after their neighbor's wife and their neighbor's land, keep their eyes closed. They will walk blind over a sorrowing road of broken whiskey bottles and greasy condoms to the boiling kettles of the damned. Unless, unless they are persuaded to open their eyes."

George, in his blindness, didn't think this message was for him. He felt cheated, the way he had the time his mama tricked him to prayer meeting by telling him it was going to be a picnic. When the Major asked him, "Do you want to help?" he answered back, "Help what, sir?" "Help save these lost souls. Do you?" George said yes because he feared to say no. The Major let go George's shirt and pondered a time with himself: "Sons of Ham, sons of Ham. Why not? They are the most sinful. They are lowly and would shame the others. Why not?" To George he asked, "Do you belong to a church?" George nodded. "What church?" "The Gilead Assembly of the Joyous Baptized, sir." "We'll go there tomorrow," the Major said. "To the *church?*" "To the church."

Then the Major explained his idea. The next day was Sunday. The two of them was to go to the Gilead Assembly and the Major would speak to the congregation, telling them to hide their sins behind four walls no longer, but to go out in the broad sky and bare them to the world, meeting the Lord and their fellow man with naked heads, as the Scripture says. This wasn't going to be talk; the Major would lead the open sinners in a parade that would win others to expose themselves.

George heard, but did not believe, until the Major said, "I appoint you my chief deputy. You will bear the banner of the saved. You are one of the sons of Ham. You will go before them with the word that I am among them, and help explain why I have come. Now I want you to learn a speech to say . . . " The idea of being a deputy with a banner and making a speech scared George, but scared him in the same stirring manner that his first meeting with the Major had done. As the Major thought up words George said them afterwards, memorizing them. They were big, church words, but since they were going to be his words, he nursed them sweet in his mouth. After he had recited a while the Major left, telling him to wait in the barn some more. George was so full of his speech he did not think to ask about food. But later in the day he crept off to his house and got his Sunday clothes and some food when his mama was out at the grocery store. He came back to the barn and sat telling his speech to the horse until dark and he fell asleep.

The church of the Gilead Assembly of the Joyous Baptized was at the edge of town on a patch of clay soil that was too poor for cotton or even grazing grass. It had no fence around it and in bad weather Mr. Gillentine's cows would shelter inside it. Mr. Gillentine owned the ground, so nobody complained or built a fence. The building had twice burned down, one way or another, and this third try was shoebox-shaped with a flat roof and no floor. A wood cross wrapped with tin cut from a Coca-Cola sign stuck out of the top. The church was kept in fresh whitewash, inside and out, though, by the backsliders Reverend Dawkins put fear of God in.

George stood at the open church door that Sunday morning with his banner in his hand. It was a shiny satin banner, dark blue on one side and orange on the other. There was orange lettering on the blue side announcing the Texas Exposition for 1936, but it had tassels and looked pretty good at the end of the hoe handle George had it tied to. The congregation was standing and singing, with their backs to George, and Reverend Dawkins, who was at the head of the aisle, had his eyes closed while he kept time by shaking a tambourine. The air was fog-white and rippling around the ceiling light bulb, like the voices were chipping off flakes of whitewash. For the first time George realized his mama and all his neighbors were in the church. He was stuck to his shoes until he watched old Dawkins' belly bouncing up and down, pumping sweat out of his bald peanut head. He thought of the times the Reverend had shamed him before his mama for not being a proper son; he thought of them and he marched down the aisle between the benches with his banner, right among the worshipers. He stood beside old Dawkins and staked his pole in the ground before anybody noticed him. They might not have noticed him for a good while had not his pole scraped the corns on the preacher's foot and made him drop the tambourine and howl.

"It's Mrs. Little's boy," one of the good sisters cried. "He's seen the Light and come to tell of his salvation."

"Great Godamighty!" another shouted. Reverend Dawkins didn't say anything, but just hopped up and down on one foot, barely keeping from cussing.

George saw his mama move to come catch him, then hold back. He decided to start his speech before he lost nerve. "My people," he declared in the deepest voice he could reach, "as the Scriptures say, no incense can purify a sinful soul, but the sun shines on the sinner's bowed head. I come to bring you out in the sun. I come to announce a man who'll tell you better than me the truth. I was wandering in the world with a heavy burden until this man eased my mind. I urge you to listen to him. As the Scriptures say . . ." He forgot what the Scriptures had said and stood there stammering a second. It gave the people a chance to catch their wits and they began to mumble. But before they could grab him or he could run away, Major Carling rode right down the aisle on his horse, and at a fast clip, too. He reined to a halt, making Reverend Dawkins scramble to the side to keep from being hit. A couple of women shrieked. The Major sat still until the hooraw stopped, his black suit and hat making him look like a messenger dropped from the skies, or popped out of the earth. "You black sinners," he said, "why are you sitting here? Do you think these flimsy walls will hold off the wrath of the Almighty God? Out, I say, out, every one of you! Bare your blighted souls to the open air. As the Scripture says . . ." And while the Major recited Holy Writ to prove his point George sneaked a glance to see what old Dawkins was making of this. The Reverend was loose-mouthed and sweating, but his eyes scrunched up when he heard the Scripture. George got the feeling then that maybe the Major was putting his own words to the Bible. George looked to see if the congregation was thinking the same.

But their faces reflected back at him a vision that changed George's life. He knew most of the people there, and yet he didn't know them at that moment. Faces that had had tired and mean straight-up-and-down wrinkles in them, those wrinkles were round and smooth like a puddle rocks were being dropped in. Toothless old mouths unsnapped and puckered like babies'. And the young folks, too, had lost their sleepy looks and were big-eyed. Young men his own age had their hair on edge, and girls were breathing short and quick. One or two of the girls were watching him, George, instead of the Major. George knew then he had learned a secret: he was saved — the Major had saved him! He saw that these people were charmed by the Major because he had an idea which he came among them of his own free will to share with them. They had been waiting all their lives for somebody —

a white man they never dreamed would — to give them a touch of hope and glory. Not just a preacher, because everybody knew a preacher talked for pay. If *he* had been on that horse they would have listened to him, George knew. His knees quivered at thinking how wrong he had been all this time, with the ideas he had had, to keep them to himself.

But when the Major finished his talk by telling all of them to follow him out into the street, marching and shouting their sins, there was a dragging of feet. The Major took some time in pulling his horse around to head it toward the door. It gave a space for an old man to squeak: "I remember chopping cotton for a quarter a day on the Carling place. This sounds like a quarter-a-day invitation to me." Reverend Dawkins picked up this tune, but he did not dare insult a white man to his face. He said, "Yes, brother, much as we enjoy the honor of this offer we must meditate on it. I suggest we pray." George saw his mama and most of the old folks nod their heads up and down. Then a long lean country man called out, "I remember last July we tried to hold an outdoor revival and Sheriff Jones stopped us because we was disturbing the peace. We got a chance to go outdoors now and we got a white man with us to ward off the sheriff. I'm tired of bending my knees in this dirt. I say, let's go."

At this instant the Major and his horse pushed off. And George picked up his pole and marched after him with a proud strut. Out of his new sense of understanding he began to sing a hymn song at the top of his voice. He couldn't remember any hymns to sing, so like the Major with the Scripture, he made up one that sounded like one. "I'm toting my troubles up a tiresome trail, I'm toting my troubles up a tiresome trail, I'm toting my troubles up a tiresome trail." That's the way it went, and it decided the congregation. The young people spilled out of the benches and followed George, then came a goodly number of the old people, everybody singing George's hymn. Reverend Dawkins and his mama and some others hung back, but George was just as glad for that. This was his event.

The Major rode along slow and stiff, not looking to the left or right to see how many was with him. He led them down the road to Congotown where most of the Negro shanties stood. Their singing and shouting made the gummy eyes of many a midnight rambler peer out of dark windows, but though George called to them and waved his banner, only one woman in a kimono came to her door and asked what was happening. "We are walking our sins away," he said. "I'd end up in China if I did that," she said and went back inside. A few hound dogs was all that joined up with the procession.

After about a mile the Major came to the big oak that separated Congotown and the white section and turned his horse around. George stood fast, making his banner a marker for the others to turn on in good order. He felt fine as the young men swung past, serious and soldierlike, and the girls in their bright dresses skipped by, throwing hot looks at him, and the old ones nodded in respect to him. It was here that the parade blocked the cars of four-five white families on their way to church.

Some marchers checked their steps as though to let the white people pass, but George held firm, feeling that this was too important for such courtesies. The white people weren't mad, though. He heard one white man call out from his car to another, "Look at what old Carling is up to now. He's saving all our nigras." And the other laughed and said, "I hope that keeps him too busy to come plaguing us with his leaflets. His daughters do their best, but I nearly signed papers to get him locked up, after he bothered folks at Mary Sue's wedding."

The marchers went back down the road to the church. When they reached it the Major gave no sign of his thinking, but turned around again and headed toward Congotown. George took his stand again to mark the turn, but he was puzzled. There was grumbling, too, among the people. Some who had come along to show off their finery didn't want to spoil it by walking some more. The more serious ones said that since no sinners had been brought to the fold in Congotown, there wasn't no sense in going back. About ten of the forty of them dropped out. George kept the singing going, though, and all went right until they reached the big oak a second time. The Major, there, pointed across to the white people's houses and said his first words: "Now we'll show them." Then he kicked his horse straight ahead, moving from the dirt road to the asphalt. Fifteen more marchers dropped out right there.

George was mystified for true. He did not hit up any singing; he was wrestling too hard with his fear. Each tall white house they passed seemed to raise its eyebrows and frown. George knew that even on Sunday mornings there was somebody left behind from Sunday school to keep watch through the blinds. The sighing of the tree branches overhead sounded like voices on the telephone wire giving news of their march. The Major looked bound for the courthouse square, for sure. The crunch-crunch of feet on the paving dwindled to a shush-shush, and then down to where all you could hear was the clack-clack of the horse's hoofs, sounding like rifle shots at midnight. The Major reached the courthouse square, and he stopped to decide if to go left to the Methodist church or right to the Baptists. He turned right. George saw a crowd of white people waiting for them, and a tickling at the back of his neck told him there was no more marchers behind him any more.

He started to run away himself, but he was held by the desperate thought that if this failed he would have nothing left, because he had given up his regular life for this. Maybe the Major could win over these white people, just as he had done the Gilead Assembly of the Joyous Baptized. Maybe even these white people would see the truth in him, George — though that was asking a heap. But maybe they, too, were waiting for a new idea and would hear it from a black man's lips. So George took a grip on the sweaty banner pole and set his gaze on the white strip of collar between the Major's black coat and red neck.

Step by step they moved forward, and the white people in their church clothes ringed in around them, not saying a thing. Sliver-glimpses of their faces out the corner of George's eyes smashed his puny dream. Their faces were stone-hard and cut with lines no words could melt. The men's bodies were hard and tight, too, almost ready to bust out of their coats and neckties. The only soft thing to be seen was the two Carling sisters off to the side, sobbing against each other like two wet sparrows.

Sheriff Jones stood in the way of the horse. He had his pistol belt strapped on over his coat like he had put it on in a hurry. The Major stopped. "You sinners," he shouted, but he got no farther in his speech. A man reached up and pulled him from the horse, and two others caught his arms, to keep him from hitting the ground and to hold him. At the same time somebody knocked the banner from George's hands.

"You ought to've known you couldn't do *that,* Major," the sheriff said slow and sad.

The Major hung between the two men with his head flung back and the whites of his eyes bulging like he was trying to die. Then he kicked out sideways and hit one of the men on the hip. They let him fall on his face in the street. He pushed and clawed with his hands and feet to try and get up, but his bad leg wouldn't give him support and all he did was scuttle along, butting into people and spitting on the asphalt. He looked like a roach that had been half stepped on and nobody could bring themselves to touch. Only when he hunched up on his side and kicked just a little bit did they lay hands on him again.

In the commotion George stopped only to bend down and tear the banner from the pole and stuff it in his pocket. Then he ran away from that town, to carry his vision to the world outside.

"This George-boy, he heading North with his message for the people?" the Spook asked sly-like when Teacher-Man stopped talking. "He is," Teacher-Man said. "Might he be on this train?" the Spook poked again. Teacher-Man just looked at his shoes and wiggled his shoulders. "Man, we carrying a high-power cargo of holiness. I hope we don't hit no bumps," the Spook joshed.

"We're liable to get splashed all over with fresh-dropped glory," Sam said, to join the teasing.

"You plan to tell the Yankee folk the same old stuff you told us?" Good-Rocking Poppa asked. "Those Yankees are too smart for corn-pone stump-shouting. They going to laugh you blue."

Teacher-Man made no reply. He dropped his head and Sam saw him squinch his eyes and push a big tear along his nose. Despite his big talk, he was just a boy, Sam realized. They oughtn't to have punched his bubble like that. The Woman acted like she saw the same thing, too. She shoved Poppa away from her so hard he banged his head on the boxcar side wall, and spoke up to Teacher-Man's rescue: "You smart bastards just better hope the Birmingham police don't unload the cargo and you along with it. What makes you think anybody's getting a prize when your lousy hides crawl out on the avenue? Boy, you still got your banner, ain't you?" she asked Teacher-Man. He patted his coat pocket. "Well, you keep that banner. Maybe your way of thinking is a little old-timey right now, but if you want to lead your people, you'll find places to lead them and right words to say, after you've been around a while. God knows, there's enough needing to be led."

Poppa moved back beside the Woman and reached out for her bosoms to make up to her. He was drunk for fair. She brushed him off and kept on talking. This is the story she told.

The Woman's Story

YOU ALL HEARD about a dog, which had a good reputation; well, this is about a cat that nobody thought much of. Of course, nobody thinks much of any cat. A cat is a cat. But part of being a cat lies in not giving a damn what anybody thinks, or at least not showing it — so the deal evens out. Down an alley in the middle of town, or on a cushion in a parlor, a cat sits light, cleaning up its own mess and taking lip off no man, living hard, loving hard, dying hard.

Marie Broussard was a cat, a born cat. She didn't have to be one — her daddy had an insurance-collection business and treated his family okay. So since she became one, it must have been bred in her.

When Marie was on summer vacation after her first year in

high school she kicked up a fuss around home about not having enough spending money to enjoy herself with. Her mama finally allowed her to take an elevator-operator job in a big downtown office building. And she had herself a ball, for a while. The place was air-conditioned, so she could dress up in her pretty-pretty duds every day and not muss them. The white people in the offices would ask her to fetch Cokes for them and give her one for doing it, so she got to drink a dozen or more bottles a day. And her boy friend, Alexander, was a delivery boy for a print shop and came in and out the building. She liked the chance to see him and tease him.

Alexander wanted to be a prizefighter. Soon as he'd have a minute free he would run over to a hole-in-wall gymnasium and pound on a punching bag or skip a rope. Marie liked the idea of having a sweetie who had such ambition, but she was a cat. She would always devil him, especially since right then she was making as much money as he was, and had more to spend, because he was supporting himself in the world.

"Well, champ," she'd say to him when he boarded the elevator with packages, "I see you bringing some more autographs for your fans. When's your next bout?"

"Now you lay off," he'd grouch, his long chin way down on his chest. He was more than six foot tall, with big bones to show where the flesh would go when he finished growing. "Are you going with me to the picture show tonight?"

"I don't want to interfere with your training. Besides, I don't get paid till day after tomorrow." She deviled him good, all right, but not ever so hard that he didn't bounce back.

The thing that ruined Marie's summer job looked like a good thing when it first popped up. There was this white girl, Sarah Rupp. Sarah worked in one of the offices, typing. She wasn't an ugly woman, best as Marie could judge the looks of somebody white and who was something older than her. She might have been too pale and sad faced, but she had a slim figure and red hair.

Sarah didn't leave with the rest of the girls at coffee-break times. At noon she went to eat by herself, since none of the sporty guys ever asked her. The usual thing was for Marie to take down a big load of people at the rush hours, then make a trip back up to get Sarah. Since the two of them rode in the elevator alone so much they started talking more than ordinary. The white girl began the conversations, and she tried to make jokes the way the usual run did. She'd kid about Marie's supposed-to-be boy friends or about how she guessed Marie had had a big time over the weekend, and such. But where other whites just joshed to make themselves look bigger, Sarah showed true interest, almost at times like she was admiring Marie.

So when Sarah asked Marie one day if she wanted to go to the movies with her, Marie was surprised — but not as surprised as she would have been at anybody else asking. All the same, she had to say the truth: "There ain't no movie places where we two can go together."

Sarah didn't back down. "Well, take a walk in the park, then."

"Park may look green, but it's all-white."

"A walk along the streets?"

Marie recognized that this white girl was awful hard up for companionship, but still, since it was a white girl, her fancy tickled up at the chance of being top dog. She set her terms: "If it's the streets in my section it might be okay."

They took their little walk on a nice starry night that was hot but had a little breeze. Marie met Sarah at the streetcar stop and steered her through the blocks where people would least likely be out on their stoops cooling themselves. They got to talking about movie stars and dance tunes and clothes, and found themselves so agreeing in taste that Marie forgot to steer, not caring where they went or who saw them. Then Sarah asked, "Where can we get a Coke?" They were just a half block from the Bull Drugstore — it took its name from the chewing tobacco sign painted on one of its sides. Marie thought twice, but her easy feeling was such that she took the white girl there.

The Bull did most of its business in selling shots of cherry tonic over the counter, but they had tables for pop drinkers, too. The girls got their drinks and would have sat and refreshed themselves without more than a soppy stare or so from the other customers, except it turned out to be Visitors' Night.

First in was Alexander, come to buy a pack of gum. Marie sat tight to let him come and go like a stranger, not knowing how to handle him and her white friend together. But Sarah saw him and sang out, "Isn't that your sweetie, the one who's always around the building?" So Marie was obliged to call him over, and he stood shifting from one foot to the other, his chin scraping his belly button, until Sarah invited him to a chair beside them. Sarah did practically all the talking, saying how she had heard Alexander wanted to be a boxer and wasn't that exciting; and though she hadn't seen many fights, there must be a lot of money in the business, and on and on. Alexander didn't know whether to say Yes ma'am or Goddamn, and Marie squirmed a little because, if it hadn't been a white girl talking, she would have sworn Sarah's words were fisherman words like girls use to hook other girls' boy friends.

But the situation never had time to clear itself. Two more visitors came into the Bull. They were policemen — a short, hefty sergeant named Paefke and a skinny patrolman named Toolen. Marie didn't know their names then, but she got to know them plain enough later. They sniffed around the place in general fashion, like they had just dropped by to remind the Bull's owner that his protection money was due. When they saw Sarah's red hair they perked up. They bumped noses, then marched over to the table and leaned over the backs of the chairs. They didn't say anything, but naturally they put the lid on the talking that had been going on. Marie looked to Sarah to speak the word that would send the officers on their way, but the white girl sat sick-scared. Alexander was digging himself a hole in the air to crawl through. So Marie spoke: "Can we help you, officers?"

"What the hell are you three doing?" the sergeant asked.

"We drinking Coca-Colas."

There was a kind of splash at Marie's words, like she had dropped a big cow-patty on the floor. Everybody looked down; it wasn't what she said but how she said it. The young cop stepped back, wanting to leave. "Come on," he said, "let's go where *we* can get a drink."

But the sergeant was swole up. "We're going all right, and they're coming with us."

"Why? Why bother with them?"

Sergeant Paefke didn't explain. His round little eyes bounced from Marie to Sarah and back, and his lips sort of rubbed hands together. Marie didn't know much, but she thought she knew what the look on his monkey face meant. Then he made a sarcastic speech: "Toolen, you'll never make the grade on the force. Don't you know we get paid for stopping things from happening as much as for what does happen? Use your imagination, boy. What does this look like to you? You want your sister coming to places like this? You got to keep the crud down, boy, or it'll flood right through your bedroom door. We're taking these three to the station. Besides, I *know* the white gal, there."

The Bull had emptied itself around them like somebody had

pulled a flushing chain, and the feeling of being deserted cooled down Marie much as anything. She and Sarah and Alexander went off in the patrol car meek as mice. At the station they were shoved through the bright lights of the photograph and fingerprint room, and then into the dim of the question room. Paefke left them to stand while he hung up his hat and unloosened his tie. He wasn't wearing a coat, since it was summer, or he would have taken that off, too. He acted like he was getting ready for a nice evening of reading the newspaper and listening to the radio. He sat down at a little desk while Toolen minded the door. There was one empty chair by the desk and he waved Alexander over to it.

"What's your real name, nigra?" Paefke asked.

"Alexander Johnson, sir, the way I told you."

"You work?"

"Delivery boy."

"Is that all you do?"

"I'd like to be a boxer if I could."

The sergeant broke out in a bunch of fat grins when he heard that. His lips grinned and the bags around his jaw joined in. He said, "A boxer, eh. Well, don't you know it's bad for your wind to chase after white women? You'd better stick to your little brown whore. Or were you acting cute tonight?"

Alexander straightened himself and met Paefke eye to eye. He was scared enough and mad enough to speak clear and bold: "Look, sir, I chased nobody, nor have you right to call Marie names. She's a high school student and respectable. Nothing done tonight deserves us this jail."

Paefke nodded his head and pulled from his pocket a finger ring, a broad banded thing with a jade stone. Everybody stared at it, wondering what it meant. "You like the girl, then," he said. "So that's why you stole the ring to give to her."

"I never saw that ring before," Alexander swore.

"Spread your hand on the desk. Go ahead, put it there," Paefke said. Alexander did. "Now remember how I asked you to let me see it back in that drugstore, but you refused me, so I had to do — *this!*" Quicker than anybody could see, he pounded down on Alexander's knuckles with a blackjack. Alexander let out a scream that was like a whistle. And he was so shocked he left his hand lay and the policeman got in another lick, harder even than before.

"I thought that'd ring a bell," Paefke said real cool. "Now get the hell out of here before I really show you something."

Alexander ran, holding his hand like it was afire. "Let him go?" the young policeman Toolen asked.

"Let him go," Paefke said. "He ain't what I have in mind. Anyway, when we take this to court it's better the judge should use his imagination about the big black buck we found threatening Miss Rupp."

Toolen was puzzled, but Marie, for sure, saw trouble plain and set herself to try escape, measuring how to get past the patrolman, looking for a window to jump out. The sergeant called up Sarah next. She walked to the desk, nervous stiff but with some color of anger in her face. She didn't sit down. He asked her, "Just what were you doing, Miss Rupp, with two nigras in a nigra place — you a white girl and them all black?"

"What are *you* doing, beating on everybody?" Sarah talked back at him. "Marie and me had been taking a walk — she runs the elevator where I work. There wasn't any place else for us to go. We were resting when her boy friend happened by. That's all. You got no right to think up a filth out of this, and bully people with your big badge. I want a lawyer. You have to let me call a lawyer."

Paefke laughed, sounding like water going down a basin drain. "I thought I remembered you, redhead. Now I know

I do. You want a lawyer. You want the one who got nol prossed the thievery charge the shipping company brought? Or you want me to telephone the old gent whose till you tapped while he was squeezing your titties? He had you sent to the house of detention just the same, though, didn't he?"

Sarah backstepped some at that, and Marie just about chunked away all hope when she learned the white girl wasn't of much more standing than a colored, since she had a police record. "That stuff is past and hasn't no connection," Sarah said.

"It's enough to make the district attorney push any charge I would want to bring, unless you tell in court about the nigra girl and her tame ape propositioning you, until Officer Toolen and myself came to the rescue."

"Christ, christ, christ," Sarah doubled her fists and called on the ceiling. "What's the point? Who you trying to punish and for what? I hated you sons-of-bitching cops when I was guilty of something. Now I haven't done a thing, so I was right in hating — "

Paefke had stood up when she started her speech and before she could finish he whipped out his hand quick and caught her by the hair and pulled her face down across the desk. She was surprised off balance and it took a second for her to try to get up. When she tried he dusted her sharp across the rear end with his blackjack. By that time he was on the same side of the desk as she was. She yelled. "Stay there and shut up," he said and hit her again.

She shut up, until he started pulling at her clothes, her underwear. Then she made a big try to twist loose. But he was ready and popped her across the back of the neck. That woozied her enough to let him get his business started. He worked her cool, standing and smiling and talking slow. "I saw you lusting after that darky boy," he said. "I'm going to show you the stuff that makes a white man best." Sarah bucked to get him off and he laughed and whipped her bare flesh. She started begging him, promising to tell any lie about Marie and Alexander he wanted her to. He told her he knew she was going to do that, anyway, and kept on.

Marie had never seen anything like that before and it was enough to send her running for the door. Toolen caught her by the shoulder and she clawed him. He didn't seem too heart-set on holding her and she might have escaped if Paefke hadn't called for the patrolman to bring her to him. Marie stopped fighting. When Paefke pushed Sarah aside like a rag doll and told Marie to take her place, she did it without a word. Marie didn't know much about white policemen or any men at that time, but the way old Paefke seemed to be getting most pleasure out of Sarah's struggling couldn't be missed.

She let him do what he pleased, even without knowing what to expect or where the pain would be, trying to keep her mind stuffed with cotton like she was in a dentist chair. He must have guessed she was playing possum, because he used the blackjack on her all the same. He needn't have. Despite the padding of her thoughts, he drilled a sore she kept.

When Paefke told her to get up from the desk, Toolen said, "Do we let them go now?" The sergeant was rumpled and sweaty from his chores and he had to suck in wind a couple times before he could chew Toolen out. "Hell no," he told him. "Let them go and they'd go claim something out of line happened to them. Charge them, and people'll figure they're lying to defend themselves. Besides, a case like this might show the judge and a few others what we're up against. Or do you want the holy-joes to put some jig sergeants on the force for you to work with? Take the nigress to a cell. Me and Miss Rupp are going to write out a complaint."

Toolen took Marie down the hall, talking to himself. She

wasn't listening at the time but she heard it to remember later. He said, "I wonder if the pension's worth it. I'm tired of tracking nigras and being scared of razors in every alley. I'm no good at seeing where a little thing could lead to trouble, watching for thinking as well as for doing. This is just like the army, this is, only they don't admit it's war. And I used to think that on the force you led parades and snitched apples." He didn't seem meant to be a good policeman, though of course he could have been sour at having to watch the sergeant take his pleasure while he wasn't allowed to have none.

The night went by slow in the jail. Marie lay on the canvas bunk like a stale sandwich, her dead body wrapped around the hollow sick feeling inside her. She felt too far away from her folks at home to even think about them. But they came the next morning, along with a lawyer named Mr. Dawkins, a Negro man. Her mama kept moaning about how she should never have let Marie take the elevator job, and her daddy was insisting to the lawyer that pandering was for men and so they couldn't hold her. Pandering was the charge that Paefke had figured out.

Lawyer Dawkins was bald-headed and gray-skinned, like he had been washed over and worn smooth by the troubles of the world. But though he hunched down, shrunk-up in his clothes, his eyes were big and alive like headlights. He sort of handled Marie's parents with each of his hands while he talked to her. "I tell you this," he said. "I know you were just larking but now this white girl is accusing you. The judge, he counts a white woman's word heavy. Every white woman reminds him of his mama. He thinks back to when he was a baby sitting on her lap on the stoop of the big white house, watching the darkies chop cotton. So you're a cotton-chopper, automatic, once he sees you. You understand? And you recognize how serious this is?"

Marie nodded her head. She didn't give too much weight to his words because she thought she knew better than him the seriousness. But she appreciated his being on her side instead of yipping at her like her mama and daddy did. Lawyer Dawkins blinked his eyes and asked, "They didn't harm you in there, did they? Bother you or anything?" Marie said no, with her eyes looking off at the clerk who was fixing the bond papers. She didn't want to explain to anybody her shame. She was trying to turn it into a secret pride, like she had been the only Negro woman in the world to be wronged in jail.

And when Alexander came around to her house later, she used it to lord over him. Of course, that wasn't hard, because she had seen him shamed and he was sheepy. "Marie, you free now?" he said real happy when he first saw her.

"I got a paper here that says I'm free, that's more than I had before I went to jail."

"I shouldn't have run when he broke my hand, but there was so much pain." He patted the plaster cast he was wearing. "I ran all the way to the river and dipped it. The moon and the water was cold and I was scared, until the city lights in the black ripples looked like blood on Negro skin. The trolley and car noises sounded mad. My fist, it swelled so big I felt myself strong enough to smash the jailhouse down. I started to go back but then I fainted."

"You didn't miss much. And heck, when you look at it, me and Sarah asked for trouble when we sneaked our walk. We should have stood in the noon sun. In daylight they couldn't have made anything wrong except in their own heads."

Marie spelled it out bold. She had all the answers. And Alexander was impressed. "You're acting mighty grown-up-like," he said.

"I've grown," she said. "I've been to school, I've been to

jail; a girl should learn to be a woman then. I'm walking slow from here on, but I ain't stepping off the walk. I'm talking low, but having all my say."

Then he surprised her by catching her arm with his good hand and declaring, "Marie, let me walk with you. I guess I've lost my job and my hopes of boxing ain't much now. But I could earn our living if you'd be the fighting fist they busted. Living together and loving together we'll lick anything. Marie, will you marry me?"

The idea sounded good to her. She didn't see how her life could be the same as before, and this offered a change. She kissed him, her lips on his forehead since his eyes were on his shoes, and she said, "What else did you think I'd ever do? I'll make you chicken stew and patch your shirts. Our child will be the first to live in style on White Folks' Avenue."

It didn't turn out that way. Her parents wouldn't hear her; they said to wait a couple years — they had enough mess now paying for a lawyer without hiring a preacher too. They thought what she should do was take up attending church more regular and prove to the neighbors she hadn't done any wrong. But Marie couldn't settle down. Instead of minding her school studies or singing in the choir, she'd slip out and go sleep around with Alexander. The things Sergeant Paefke had done made her want to get even, kind of, and to rub out the feeling he had left. She took up smoking, too, though that didn't have any connection directly.

The only person suspicioning what Marie was doing was Lawyer Dawkins. He would call her to his office and ask her to tell over and again what had happened at the police station. She never answered the truth. He'd smile dry then preach a little. "Look," he'd say, "I'm an old man who had his chance to catch the scraps from the table of them eating high on the hog, but I picked the lean rocky road. And I've walked too far now with a sack of wildcats on my back to worry about anything but flowers for my grave. You want to fight this case or don't you?"

"I ain't no petunia," Marie answered smart-alecky.

"No, you *ain't*. And that makes you one of the ones who ought to want most for the law to be fair. Preachers don't care what kind of policemen the city's got; *they* not likely to be spending their evenings in the pokey."

She knew he was teasing her by pretending to believe she was bad, and she played a game with him. But she knew he was serious in wanting to get at the police and she admired him trying, even if she didn't intend to help. She listened to him talk about the NAACP and the organizations for Negroes' rights. When he offered her an after-school job of doing typing at his office, she wanted to take it. But then she got hooked in a family way.

It was after she had missed three periods she decided what it was. She told Alexander and he whooped it up for eloping and getting married. But when it turned out he didn't have the money in pocket for a license and blood test, she decided on just *telling* her folks she and Alexander had got married, and while they were fussing she packed some clothes and left. She might have been half hoping that the road for her to come back home would be open, when they found she wasn't really married. On that same day Lawyer Dawkins told her he had buffaloed the district attorney into dropping charges, since Marie was under age, but the police hadn't taken her to the juvenile bureau like they were supposed to. He must have been disappointed that she didn't raise more enthusiasm for the news.

Alexander found him a job as a prize-ring handyman at the Little Gypsy. The Little Gypsy was a combination night club and gymnasium. The bar lay in front, the gym in the back — and at night they rolled away the stuff to make a dance floor of it. There were furnished rooms upstairs and Marie and Alexander moved in. She started working as a waitress and learning how to drink liquor.

The Little Gypsy didn't ever close and enough went on twenty-four hours around to make it unneedful to step outside the walls. Marie liked watching the fighters pumping and sweating while the gamblers bunched together talking chances. Then at nightfall the working men would come by for their beers before supper and make a lot of sassy talk with the waitresses before going home to their wives for supper. After them, the nighttime ramblers gathered, the men and women pairing off the way they felt like, some dancing to the music of the piano, some making love talk, some just drinking. The doings looked new and romantic to Marie. What's more, the boss of the place, an Italian fellow named Louie Castro, didn't mind what the waitresses sipped out of the bottles so long as they stayed around to help at rush times. Marie fooled around, getting buzzes on three-four times a day, just to enjoy the dizzy feel.

Alexander hit it off high and handsome, too. He landed work with a sizable stable of fighters and was kept busy with the liniment bottle and the water bucket all day. After the training had done, the gamblers buddied up to him to ask his opinion about one boy and the other. Maybe he'd be sent along to be chaperon for a fighter going to the movies or someplace. He felt mighty big and busy and didn't spend much time with Marie. But she didn't mind, she was enjoying herself being barmaid. And on the nights of the fights, she got a pass to sit in the front rows of the arena and look important. They were traveling light, Alexander and Marie, so light they almost forgot her little burden inside.

When it came the time where she had to do or don't, she

didn't. They decided she should go see the midwife. So their first child was flushed down the toilet bowl.

A short time after that, Alexander brought company to the room with him, along with a big bottle of Scotch whiskey. It was a lightweight fighter named Killer Jackson. He fought main events, this Killer did. He stood shorter than most he boxed against, since his heft was all in his arms and shoulders and neck. The visit surprised Marie. The barroom downstairs was usually their parlor for meeting people. But she played the hostess, rinsing out the toothbrush glasses for them to drink out of and sitting on the bed while the men sat on the room's two chairs. Nobody had much to talk about. Alexander counted his toes while Killer, with his flat face and droopy eyelids, could have been a frog looking for flies on the ceiling. They drank the whiskey straight and Marie helped herself good to the Scotch's smoky taste. Soon she was chattering away like a squirrel.

Then Alexander got up and said he was going out for a pack of cigarettes. Killer said something about it being about time and Alexander left. Hardly had the door clicked shut than Killer caught Marie around the shoulders and pushed her back flat on the bed. He took the glass out of her hand and began to hug her and tear at her clothes. She was surprised and dizzy. When she pushed against him he crushed her with his muscles. She tried to holler but he choked her off with his thumb on her throat. He did his business fast and hard, not saying a word. They lay on the bed afterwards. Marie couldn't think what to do.

She heard Alexander's footsteps in the hall and moved to pull her dress down and sit up. But Killer didn't stir and he pushed her back flat with his arm. And Alexander knocked on the door, instead of walking in. "Did you get me a pack of cigarettes, too?" Killer asked lazy-like. "No," said Alexander from outside. "Then go get me one," the fighter told him. And Alexander went. Killer worked Marie over again. Then he stood up, tucked in his shirt and was about to leave with his bottle of whiskey under his arm when Alexander came back and made some more mouse taps. This time Marie spoke out, calling him inside. She didn't try to straighten her clothes.

Alexander didn't look at her, but held out the pack of cigarettes stiff and stupid. Killer didn't even take them, but brushed on by with a "Be-seeing-you." Alexander sniffed around the room, nose down like a hound dog, searching for the bottle that wasn't there any more. Then he gave up and began undressing for bed, still not meeting her eyes. She studied him close, though. She tried to believe he actually didn't know anything out of order had happened while he was out. But his knocking at the door spoiled that. She still stopped short of blaming him. After all, they weren't really married and maybe some of the men downstairs had been teasing him about being stuck with her, and Killer Jackson had dared him to give him a chance at her. Alexander might have been teased into doing it, figuring Marie could take care of herself — and she should have been able to, if she hadn't drunk so much. So she put herself at fault and didn't say anything. But the next day she went out and bought a little pistol at a hock shop.

Marie and Alexander flitted around in their usual style for a few days. A fight night came up and Marie and another waitress went on their passes. They sat in their finery, acting dignified and important, while the fans pushed back and forth through the aisles, buying their beer and placing their bets. The bouts went along as usual except the white policeman patrolling the arena looked like Officer Toolen and that unsettled Marie. When things were over, Marie stood by the door of the dressing room waiting for Alexander to finish with his chores. They usually went out and ate boiled crabs after fight nights. But this night he brought with him the fighter who had been in the last bout. Cha-Cha Kid, he called himself. He had won, but he had took a pasting. His face had adhesive tape up and down it and one eye was pooched and purple. He didn't even nod at making Marie's acquaintance but kept on talking to Alexander. "The guy wasn't a dirty fighter, the way I expected," he was saying with his lips stiff like he had memorized a piece. "I thought he'd fold up, the way most old guys do, if I kept downstairs on him. Left, left, right, I went but he had a tough gut so I changed."

Cha-Cha Kid was broadcasting his fight over again and Marie didn't want to spend the rest of her evening with a punchdrunk. She tugged at Alexander for them to go get their crabs by themselves. But Alexander said bright-like, "How about us all going up to the room and relaxing over some drinks in quiet?" Marie understood. She didn't answer yes or no. She went along in the cab, waiting while they stopped at the liquor store for a bottle and thinking about if anybody could tell a pistol was unloaded by looking at it. At the room she poured into the glasses and sat on the bed — and waited. Cha-Cha Kid skated around the floor, acting out every punch. When he was almost through with the last round, Alexander stood up. "I'm going to go get some Cokes for mixers," he said. "This stuff is too raw to go down naked."

"Just a minute," Marie said. He waited while she went over to the dresser. She took her pearl-handle pistol from the drawer, shook it in her fist and told: "Since you going, you better take your clothes with you. And take this bum, too. He don't need a whore, he needs a nurse."

"What you mean?" he asked. But his head was down; he knew.

"Did they make that part of your job, supplying a woman for the fighters?" she gave him straight.

"You didn't complain before."

"You planned it then, before. You wanted it to happen and then were going to kid me into it regular. If you wanted to pass me around like a deck of cards you ought to have been the man to tell me about it."

He clinched his hands open and shut fretting what to do and Marie saw the baggy lump across his knuckles that Paefke had left. That made her mad in a way that left her not able to bawl him out more. She could just wave the gun and tell him over and again to git.

Alexander started packing his things, messing her clothes around while he did it. "You didn't raise no kick about these when I bought them for you," he fussed. Cha-Cha Kid bobbed up and down, his head tilted like he was pretending to fight somebody taller than him. Marie knew the man too dumb to be following the goings on, but she wanted to make a point bad. She hit the boxer hard as she could on the side of the face with the pistol. He went down on one knee, like in the ring, and blood leaked between his bandage strips. He rattled his head to clear it and was coiling to come at her with his fists, not saying a word, not a sign of expression. Marie saw he meant to chop her to bits, cold — not even having the sense to be mad when he did it. But she held her ground and pointed the pistol snout right up between his eyes, like showing a pocket watch to a baby. She told him to get the hell out and he got.

Alexander had turned google-eyed watching this and Marie stuck it to him: "I would give you the same treat, you bastard, if you was a fighter. But you ain't no fighter, not you. You a fighter's pimp, that's all." He couldn't face her, but he talked to his suitcase, trying to pay her out. "It wasn't my idea we not get really married. I was agreeable," he said. She just told him, "Leave the bottle behind. Leave the bottle, this time." And Marie had the cork off soon as the door slammed behind him. She did that bottle in like a jug of ice tea and went down to the Little Gypsy for highballs to build up the fire.

Three days and nights she kept the fire going, laughing and joking, running around to joints over town. She was a real-gone cat. Then she woke up in bed one afternoon and thought she was dead. Her insides ached and felt choked like she was one long sore throat. Her eyes had gummed shut, her neck stabbed her brain when even she breathed. She tried to get back to sleep, but it was too bad. She turned to measure the distance to the handbasin for water — and saw the big white body in bed with her, all fat naked, its back to her. She couldn't make sense of the droopy butt ends or the belly folds that came all the way around to the backbone. She followed a black trail of hair that went up to the thick neck and recognized from the big ears and the bald patch on top the head that it was the owner of the Little Gypsy, Louis Castro.

She couldn't remember how he got there and she didn't want to think of what they must have done together. She lay there looking at him like he was a glob of something she had thrown up out of her stomach. When he stirred awake she pretended to be asleep. But after he got his clothes on he stood at the end of the bed and pulled her toe. "Once you get dried out, babe," he said, "you might as well come on down and get started. Some of the other girls'll explain how we handle the money end. I think you'll make a good little entertainer — if you start using something besides a pistol." He gave a swipe across her private parts to show what he meant and snickered while he walked out the room.

Marie felt fear mix with her sickness; the toe Castro had pulled ached like a steel band was clamped around it, chaining her to the bed. She laid still until night came — not sleeping, just lying. Then thirstiness made her get up. She pushed a little water down, swaying all over on her feet. Finally she made herself look in her purse and in the dresser. She didn't have penny-one left nor the pistol neither. She went back to bed and tried to think of pitchers of cold lemonade, but about five o'clock in the morning she got another idea. She dressed herself up good as she could and tiptoed down the stairs, hoping not to be seen. She walked the sidewalk in the direction toward Lawyer Dawkins' office. It was a long distance off, but she would still make it there too early, so she walked slow.

She passed a little downtown square park that had some benches and grass and one tree, and wanted to sit till the sun rose. But she knew that the park was for whites only, twenty-four hours a day, and feared a policeman would catch her. She went by a couple of all-night hash joints, but they were all-white, too, and she didn't have money for a toothpick, even if they weren't. Right then, with the sky not black or white, but gray like a coffin, and the streets and buildings dead and lonesome, Marie decided without thinking it that she was a cat, an alley cat. No husband or boy friend, no family, no money, no nothing except sick empty space in her belly. Her idea in going to Lawyer Dawkins had been to hint around for the office work he had offered her once. Were she to get that she would move out of the Little Gypsy and room someplace else. Then later she might go back to her mama and daddy, or let them know where she was, anyway.

That had been her idea, but even before she came on Lawyer Dawkins she knew it wouldn't work. He was sitting on a cane chair in front of the funeral parlor, getting the early sun; his office was upstairs. He didn't rise up from his chair but kept it tilted back against the wall. His big eyes looked at her like melted ice when he said, "Well, howdy, Miss Marie. I understand you're a married lady now."

It seemed to her he was reading right into her mind and

seeing how bad she felt and all that went before. But she bucked against him acting like a preacher for her sins, even if she had disappointed him before. All the blame she took was that maybe her fancy clothes were out of place so early in the day. And against him, she thought that if he had law business to amount to anything he wouldn't be out on the pavement — so the job he talked of months back must have been out of bragging or charity. Marie didn't allow him more time to mock her. She said, "Oh yes, I'm doing fine and how are you," and walked on by — right back to the Little Gypsy.

The Little Gypsy was where she stayed, for better than a year, until the Big Man thought she'd be a good entertainer at his places and he bought her. She didn't worry about nothing. Alexander had mixed in with some morphine peddlers and was long gone. The nearest to a family she had was her oldest sister, Louise, who she'd spend vacations with time and again.

Louise's husband Jack worked nights at the post office and they lived in a rent-cottage in the University section where Louise did housework for the wives of white professors who stayed all around there. Louise had her steady routine for workdays and her church for Sunday and was respectable in every way. She didn't question when Marie came. She took her in like they were still girls together playing house. Her only sharp edge showed when she wouldn't touch any of Marie's money for room and board. Jack slept most of the time he was home and didn't say anything. They had a son, Jimmy, who was starting high school and who liked Marie a lot.

Staying there usually made a nice change for Marie. Except this one particular time had its disturbance on account of Jimmy. He and another kid had been fiddling around a building project and were blamed for taking plumbing pipe. The juvenile court put him on probation instead of sending him to the Home, but natural enough the shame bit his mama hard — specially since the white social worker came by once a week to pry. Jack beat Jimmy up then washed his hands of it by hinting that the criminal blood came from Louise's side, tossing a look at Marie for his proof.

Then one day Louise told Marie a professor had asked if she knew where he could find a part-time maid, so why didn't Marie take the job. The professor offered to pay seventy-five cents an hour, eleven to five, and no cooking. Marie was used to making a lot more than that an hour and she didn't need the pocket change. Besides, she feared she might bite her tongue off if she had to bend a knee and listen to a lot of white-folk talk. But at the same time, her vacation was getting long and she figured she might as well please Louise. She said she'd go.

The University section had white and black people's houses mixed through and through like meat and gristle in a two-bit steak. Two sides of a square would be white and the other two sides black. White folks held down the four corners on the block and turned their houses' backs to their Negro neighbors. Marie went for her new job to a little shotgun bungalow squeezed between two bigger houses. She knocked on the rusty screen front door, meaning to show right off that she didn't intend to shuffle in through the back with a bandanna on her head. A stumpy old man opened up. He looked like a Chinaman, like Charley Chan. She drooped her jaw and cussed Louise for not telling her that. He said something and while she tried to make out what it was, he swept her inside with a big bow and scrape. He gave his name, which was Tatsumi and mixed her up more because it sounded Italian.

She looked around the front room of the bungalow and saw mostly books and clutter — books around the walls and papers and such on the furniture. Everything looked American, except a strong smell like manure was all over. "Very dirty, I'm ashamed," this Professor Tatsumi explained without explaining nothing. He took her to the bedroom, where there were two single beds not made up and dirty clothes hanging out of the armoire and the dresser. And more manure smell. The kitchen lay right behind, the way rooms go in shotgun houses, and when Marie saw it she felt sure of what she had begun to think: there wasn't no wife staying here. She decided to quit the job before she started.

Then a white man came into the kitchen from off the back porch. He was not much taller than Professor Tatsumi, but was younger. He had pink round cheeks and his sand-color hair was cut short, making him look like a baby rooster. He wore a T-shirt and khaki pants. "This my friend, Dr. Hastie," Tatsumi said.

This Dr. Hastie smiled and read Marie's face. "We won't expect you to clean up this mess," he said. "We'd be satisfied if you can just keep the place no worse than it is now." He sniffed his nose in the air. "As for the perfume, let me show you." He led Marie and his partner onto the porch. Cages and cages were stacked there, little cages with barely enough space between the rows for one person to squeeze through. They looked like they held baby chickens, but Dr. Hastie said, "Those there are for our cats, those for our rats and those are for both." And Marie saw the cats, plain alley cats, in one stack, and mean gray rats in another — and then in the "for both" cages were little baby kittens and rats in together, not bothering each other but looking calm as could be. Cats, rats, yellow man, white man, black woman — Marie didn't know where the merry-go-round was headed. Then Dr. Hastie said, "Don't worry, you won't have to clean the cages. That's scientific work." His voice didn't have any big-boss boom to it to ruffle her fur, so she joined the rest of the cats.

Marie began work on the dirty dishes in the sink, while Dr.

Hastie went back to carpentering on a cage in the back yard and the Professor sat on the front-room sofa and marked papers. Later in the afternoon she finished with the kitchen and straightened the bedroom. She walked into the front room with a broom, but stopped when she saw the Professor sunk down in the sofa, asleep at his work. He was still holding a paper, his glasses about to slide off his nose. He didn't look queer or spooky then, but more like an old sugar-sack doll. She wasn't going to wake him and she wasn't going to move his things around without being told — specially since he was some kind of scientist. So she decided to burn the trash she had collected and go home. She toted the trash box past the animal cages. She didn't give the cats and rats a glance. There wasn't any plain reason why they should be made a zoo of, so she didn't want to make them her business.

Out in the yard Dr. Hastie sat on the bare ground, bending over a wood cage frame, trying to hammer chicken wire on with staples. He held a tobacco pipe in his teeth almost the size of the hammer. "Come drive this damn thing in for me, Marie," he said, peeved at himself.

She set the trash down slow and came over to him slow. She was still on the lookout. But when she saw the mess he had made of the other nails he had driven in, she squatted down and fixed the staple and a couple more besides. "It's a pretty cage," she said to be saying something.

"It'll hold together, that's all," he said. "But the real part of it hasn't been built yet. Tatsumi is going to rig the doors and triggers that go inside. Wait till you see them. Me, I'm no good with my hands — I'm more of a *thinker*. S-t-i-n-k-e-r. *Thinker*." She couldn't say yes or no or maybe so to that. She got up to start her fire. He kept talking on: "Yes, I'm real thinky. I sit fooling with an animal cage while those guys out there build them for human beings. You see them?" There wasn't much room for looking. The rear ends of the big houses stuck out like blinkers on each side of the back yard. Straight ahead, to the left a little, she could see work going on at a string of little flat-top cottages. Some were finished, others had just the sides or the foundations up. They were all going to be painted blue, it seemed. It was around there that Marie's nephew Jimmy had got in trouble, but she couldn't figure what it meant to Dr. Hastie. "Those little houses ain't too pretty," she said.

"They're uglier than they look," he said. "There used to be places for Negroes to live there — shacks, but places — but they tore them down. Tell me, where are those Negroes living now?"

Marie studied him. He had asked his question like a schoolteacher wanting a straight answer. But he was white and his voice sounded white-Southern. So she didn't know if he wanted it straight. "Why, they're living in with their kinfolks, most like," she finally said.

"They're not going to be able to buy any of those new houses, are they? Those houses are going to be for white people." He was telling and not asking, so she just nodded her head and poked the fire. He stood up and talked to her back: "What Tatsumi and I are doing doesn't mean a thing against that. You saw those kittens and baby rats in the same cage — nothing to it. If you take the animals when they're young enough, they won't even learn they're supposed to be enemies. We're trying to go farther and show they can get to work together, co-operate."

"Like circus animals?" Marie asked.

Dr. Hastie laughed sour. "That's what the head of the department at the University said when we told him about it. That's why we have to do the work here instead of having laboratory space. But we aren't trying to make animals act like human beings, we're trying to shame human beings into acting like animals."

She wasn't the one to wonder at how anybody made a living. "There's probably somebody willing to pay good money for such," she said.

"We'll probably get lumps on the head for our trouble, if people find we're serious," he said.

While Marie walked home she shuffled in her mind the pieces of her first day at work. She reasoned that if she had to be a maid it was good she worked for a queer two men instead of a fancy white lady. The job was different anyhow. She was interested in it enough that when Buddy Nix drove up to the house after supper to see her she treated him like bad news.

Buddy was Marie's agent, sort of, at the places she did entertaining. He could have been a preacher, though, from the way he wore solid-color suits and specs with silver rims. He carried his thin frame stiff and even his mustache ends stuck out righteous-like. He never drove around town with the top of his yellow convertible down, neither. But he didn't cross the door sill of Louise's house. Louise had froze him in his tracks the first time he tried. He and Marie had their talk on the stoop. "The Grand Jury's gone home so the lights are bright again," he told her.

"The Big Man pass the word?" she asked, knowing in advance that Buddy never said but what the Big Man put in his mouth.

"He did for true. Go pack your bag."

"Is there a rush?"

"The johns are beating down the door to get in," he said. "Besides, we got a whole slew of all-night parties booked."

Marie didn't move. "I tell you, man, I ain't been feeling too good. I think I'll stay out a while more. I figure it's no sense killing myself. There'll always be work to be got."

"But it's been three weeks," he argued, and would have argued some more if some people hadn't come walking along. So he said, "Okay, Marie baby, catch yourself a deck of vim and vitamins and I'll drop back in a couple days." His teeth made a smile under his mustache when he said it, but his eyes had fish scales over them.

The next day when Marie walked in the cottage, Professor Tatsumi was there by himself, bright like an electric bulb with excitement. He couldn't even try to speak English. The cage Dr. Hastie had built sat on the kitchen table. Inside, a fair-size rat, a dingy gray one, was sniffing around like he had worries and didn't know where they were coming from. The cage had been divided in half by a board hanging on hinges. On the side opposite the rat a big piece of cheese lay for bait. The Professor pointed to a knob at the end of a string that looped around some pulleys and weights. Marie guessed that he wanted to make the rat yank on the knob to get the cheese. She didn't think the rat would do it, but she stood and watched — with the cage in the way, she couldn't start work, anyhow.

The rat moved its head around quick and jerky, like a wind-up toy. Marie could tell it thought it knew all about cages but was mixed up by the smell of cheese it couldn't see. It tracked the smell to the door and pushed its nose along the crack at the bottom, like looking for leaks in a gas pipe. It went back and forth, passing right under the knob, not finding how to get through. Then it got mad and began bumping its head on the door, on the cage sides and even jumping at the roof. It wore itself to a nub and laid down in a lump, twiddling its fingers. After a minute it rose up slow and took stock, going over the ground where it had made a fool of itself, like it was studying a different rat altogether. The Professor started hissing to beat a peanut whistle. The rat stood in front of the knob. Finally it said what-the-hell to itself and pulled on the string. The door swung back slick as grease. The rat didn't believe it. It wouldn't stick its nose past where the door had been, until that cheese looked just too good, and it jumped and had half of the chunk eaten in a bite. The Professor clapped his hands and said some happy sounds to himself. Then to Marie he said, "We try cat next. Then both cat and rat."

"Both?" she asked.

"They hungry, they learn to pull knobs together. Learning is to do something for hunger, that's all," he said.

"That ought to make a good show to show people."

"Yes, yes," he said, pointing his finger at her. "And people will think if cat and rat get along, why we fight, if we smarter than animal? No more war. We work together in peace, everybody."

Marie put his words together in what she thought was his idea and asked him, "But with people, what if one is hungry and the other ain't?"

He made a bulldog face. "Not food. No matter how much people eat, they hungry inside. Hungry for each other. They want each other." He was so sad-looking she was sorry she had stirred up his worry. But Dr. Hastie came in the house then to break up the seriousness. When he heard the news about the rat, he slapped the Professor on the back and fetched three bottles of beer from the refrigerator. Before Marie could think on the strangeness of it, she was sitting with the two men around the table, making a toast to the rat in the cage.

Dr. Hastie joked away about how different professors at the University would cut their throats when the tests were done. The Professor smiled like a little pumpkin. They had another beer and then the Professor bounced up at remembering he was supposed to go teach a class. Soon as he left, Marie figured the party was over and started for the sink and the dirty dishes. Dr. Hastie waved her back down to the chair and got them some more beer. "He doesn't give a damn what the University thinks about the experiment; he's aiming at the public," Dr. Hastie said about his partner. "All that's important to him is stopping another world war. He's single-track on the idea — and he's got a right to be. His wife died in a concentration camp during the last one."

Drinking in the early afternoon set Marie dizzy, specially since she was out of practice. She swore off when she stayed at Louise's. So she was relaxed and forgetful of her place. She felt like a lady of the house — not a house woman — in the kitchen, even though the face opposite her was white and there was a rat on the table. She thought of what she knew about concentration camps and came right out with what she didn't understand: "But Professor Tatsumi ain't Jewish, is he?"

"It was an *American* concentration camp in Wyoming, not Germany," Dr. Hastie told her. "He's Japanese and the government moved him and his family from the West Coast right after the start of the war. He lost his teaching job, his wife and his son — his son got killed fighting in Italy, fighting on our side. That's why he might seem funny at times."

Marie hadn't considered Professor Tatsumi as being colored the same way she was colored — that is, not only skin-colored but *trouble*-colored. And she wondered at how everything was blending in. The Professor had pointed out her likeness to the rats and cats; Dr. Hastie showed the Professor's likeness to her, and now the beer was bringing Dr. Hastie in close. "And what makes you take such a big part in the scheme?" she asked him.

He laughed ho-ho, tossing his head back like a baby rooster trying to crow — except his blue eyes were squinched to show he was laughing at himself. "Me?" he said. "Me, I've lost *two* wives. They're not dead, they're just gone. They left me. They got tired of watching me beat myself over the head." This didn't lead anywhere, so Marie didn't speak. She reached for her beer bottle on the table. His hand that was holding his glass moved over and held her hand. The rat had filled his belly with the cheese and was asleep. Dr. Hastie started explaining some more: "I've lived all my life in the South, God help me. God help *any* white kid born in the South. He laps up guilty milk, and guilty candy and guilty porkchops and gets fat with guilty fat, right up to the neck. Then comes the time he has to choose between letting his brain get fat or cutting his head off. Nobody cuts his own head off. I compromise by beating on it. So if Tatsumi wants to jab society in the ass, I'm with him. Odd-ball or not, it's the only game in town, as the fellow said. The rest of the guys in my racket are studying incest among fruit flies."

His hand touching hers bothered her. She had been touched before, all right, but Dr. Hastie was reaching deep, reminding her of a long time ago. She couldn't figure what he wanted and she pulled her hand loose. Dr. Hastie left his hand lie, its palm open, asking her back. "A Negro now," he said, "a Negro has it easier — easier because it's tougher. Right from the crib he knows what he wants and who to hate. He's born angry — "

Marie didn't like this mind-reading, along with the hand-holding. It was pulling her in too close and she wanted room to jump, just in case. "Why do you tell me this?" she asked sharp. "Is it because I'm a Negro and can't do you harm by hearing it?"

He laughed ho-ho again. "You mean to say Negroes are people the same as anybody else, except they have to live by different rules?" She waited him out and he went on. "Well, you're wrong — about the rules, that is. The rules are the same for white and black; it's only the bastards who *make* the rules who want you to think they're different." He took his glass of beer and went over to the back door. "*They* make the rules," he said. "Those guys who are building those houses out there. They own the town and they play it like a checkerboard, moving black and white from one square to the other, any way they choose, any way they can make a fast buck. And they can't lose, they're playing on a nerve that everybody's got. Why once in a while even some of our brainwashed cats hear the call of the wild and eat up their buddy rats." He turned away from the door and let out a deep breath. Then he said slow, "That reminds me. If you know anybody who can get us some baby rats, we'll pay fifty cents apiece. Just plain rats."

She didn't know who *they* were out there, but the words had a fight sound she hadn't heard for a long time and didn't find bad to hear again. She was willing to decide he wasn't up to monkeyshines. And the idea hit her that she should set her nephew Jimmy to bagging rats. He'd go for making the half-dollars, and she wanted him to meet with Dr. Hastie and the Professor. He was still young enough for some of their thoughts to take root.

What is more, she worried about what the police arrest might do to Jimmy. She had made him a promise that she would pay his way to college if he kept his grades up in school — and she really had some money put by to do it, too. But with this trouble she feared the colleges wouldn't let him in. Meeting with the two professors might be as close as he was going to get. She blamed herself somewhat for Jimmy's trouble. He had a fool-kid's admiration for her, and while he might not know for sure what she did, she thought he had a good guess and was styling himself to follow her steps into the sporting life. He was smart and looked to grow handsome enough to get high in the world if he tried. But when she talked to him about his studies he laughed sly at her with his eyes like she was make-pretending interest and that they both knew he was going to strut out among the bright lights soon as he reached age.

That evening after supper when she told him about the rat-catching plan, he gave her his wise-guy look, his body crooked all sassy. "I bet that old Chink eats them rats, that's what," he said.

Marie drew back and slapped him hard across the face. "The only chinks I know are the ones I'll put in your hide if you keep slamming people you don't know anything about. They are two of the brainiest men ever. You might learn something if you keep your big mouth shut." Beating on Jimmy was his mama Louise's job and Marie hadn't ever dreamed of doing it before. The newness of her fist on the side of his head and her rough words cut him down a few pegs. The next day he was at the door of the shotgun bungalow with two dollars' worth of baby rats in an old shoebox.

Professor Tatsumi took to him like a hen to a chick, and showed him all about the experiment and taught him how to handle the animals without scaring them or getting bit. Jimmy started on his own to do Dr. Hastie's back-yard carpenter work for him, leaving the white man free to smoke his pipe and talk his mind. He talked about the new houses across the way and Jimmy listened to that. Dr. Hastie used the houses as example to show how everybody would do better, if white and black could get over their fear of each other and share and share alike. Marie would sneak off from her chores to listen to the lectures, too, and out of them she thought up an experiment of her own.

Her plan turned around Jimmy and the money for college she was nesting away for him. It had a double bull's-eye—either to help Jimmy right then by getting him a better chance to grow up decent, or to get him plenty enough money for the best kind of schooling later. She had it in mind as a test for Dr. Hastie, too. He talked nice, but now she wanted to see if he was brave enough to do right. The day they taught a cat the trick of opening the door in the cage, she put the scheme to him.

The kitten behaved itself different from the rat. It wanted the milk on the other side, but it had enough fat on its bones to be more dignified. It bumped its nose on the barrier, fussed a little, then curled up to try to sleep away the thought of the milk. But it roused itself in a short while and started moseying around again. When it reached up and pulled the knob on the string Marie couldn't tell whether it had thought something would happen or if it had taken the knob for a play-pretty. After the door opened the cat moved over to the milk calm as you please.

Professor Tatsumi and Jimmy cheered, Dr. Hastie smiled, and at this good minute Marie caught his elbow and led him aside to the bedroom. "Dr. Hastie, you don't like those new houses they're building, do you?" she asked. He puckered his face like he thought she had gone crazy. "So why don't you buy one?" she said to perk his interest some more.

"Buy one of them? Did you say *buy* one?"

"Yes," she said. "Buy one and then give it to a Negro family."

He laughed his laugh that showed he took this to be a joke on him. "Sure," he said. "That's perfect. But houses cost money. The best ideas cost money, I'm sorry to say."

"How much is first payment on a house that size?"

"About a thousand dollars, including insurance and stuff."

"I think I can get a thousand dollars. Would you buy it with that, if the family that moved in kept up the rest of the payments?"

"*You're* going to buy a house there?" he shouted out, like the sun had risen at midnight.

"Not me, personal," she said with business-style mystery.

"But I think I can promote the deal. Let me have till tomorrow and I'll learn for sure. Do you want me to do that?"

He agreed, like she expected he would, but she gave him overnight on purpose, to let there be chance for him to weaken. She could have written a check that minute, had she been sure of him. But a lot of working and cheating and lying — a lot of lying — had gone into her having that much in the bank, and she wanted to be sure.

Louise and Jack were part of the plan, too, and they had to be persuaded. That night Marie went into the kitchen at Louise's when Jack was eating his meal before going to work. It was a silent rule that Marie wasn't to be around when Jack ate, or was otherwise with Louise, so the two of them looked at her surprised. She put the idea to them straight: "How'd you like to own a house?"

Jack had a mouthful of stew. He rolled it from one side of his long, lean cheeks to the other, up and down, like it was a plug of tobacco. Then he let it rattle down his scrawny throat and said, "What kind of house do you have in mind, Sister Marie?"

"I mean a house you can buy for yourselves to live in."

"Oh, *that* kind of house. I wasn't sure," he said and took another gob of stew. It was a dirty dig and Louise glared at him for it. "What do you mean, honey? You heard of a home for sale around here?" she asked Marie.

"Right in the next block and brand-new, too."

Old Jack swallowed his food quicker this time. "Where's that?" he asked. "Over that way, on the lake side," Marie pointed. He screwed up his forehead, then solved the puzzle. "Them's for white folks," he grunted. Marie hit him with an answer before he could get to work on his plate again. "Nobody's decided whether they are for white folks yet or not," she said. "Besides, what if a white man was to do the buying and give you the deed?"

"White man? Slow down, Marie. I don't understand," Louise begged.

Marie put the cards on the table — though all of them wasn't exactly face up: "One of the professors I work for, Dr. Hastie, thinks it'd be a good investment to lend some money on a house to some family, and he don't care what kind. I mentioned you all, and one of those new houses, and he agreed, if you wanted to."

"Sounds like a hot-air notion to me," Jack scoffed.

"Suppose you get the deed, and suppose the builder don't like it. He don't want Negro folks in the middle of his shiny new houses," Marie whispered, inviting herself down beside Jack and pushing her face close to his. "So he comes to you and offers to buy his house back. And since you bought it legal there's nothing he can do but offer you twice what you paid."

That was the kind of talk Jack could understand. He wiped his lips on his handkerchief and began picking at his teeth with his finger, smiling a big-cheese smile the while. "So without putting up a penny or even moving a stick of furniture I could turn over a dollar or two? How much of the profit is this Dr. Hastie ready to give me? Tell him I want half, and I ain't signing no notes to him, in case anything goes wrong."

"I'm sure he's agreeable to that."

"Then I'm agreeable," Jack said, slapping both his palms on the oilcloth table top. "How about you, Louise?"

"If you want," Louise said, but her face was fence-post thoughtful. And later that night she started prowling around the house, looking at the wall stains the leaky roof had made and the rusty plumbing pipes and things like that; then she'd sit quiet and wrapped up, wrestling with herself. Marie didn't ask questions. She knew Louise wasn't thinking of profiting off the house purchase, she was imagining what it would be like to live in a new place instead of paying big rent for an old dump — and she was bracing herself for the trouble that trying to live in the new place would cause. The years of bending her knee on white women's floors hadn't taken all the starch out of Louise. Marie felt proud of her.

Dr. Hastie did noble, too, when Marie told him the next day that Louise and Jack were willing. He made a hand salute and said, "Which house do they want?" Marie acted like she was thinking hard before she answered: "A blue one." Since the houses were all blue, they laughed together on that. Then Marie handed him the down-payment check from her brassière. He sobered up when he took it. "Don't mention this to Tatsumi," he said. "I don't think he'd better know. Being involved in it would probably cost him his job."

"What about *your* job?"

"I'm likely not to get my contract renewed at the University, no matter what I don't do. Besides, I'm a *white* man and can drift on easier."

Marie took this as big talk. She knew from reading the Negro newspapers that people had been shot and bombed for moving into houses not meant for them, and she figured Dr. Hastie knew it, too, and wouldn't be throwing away his job unless he had an escape hole in mind. *She* had an escape hole — the selling of the house back, if it got too rough. She wondered what his was, and it worried her when he asked if it'd be all right to wait till tomorrow to buy the house. What if he cashed the check and kept the money, who'd believe her?

This worry led her to tell the Professor about the plan, mostly to make him witness to the check. He didn't understand easy — he hadn't even noticed the houses being built.

When he did catch the idea, it hit him hard. He let the book he was reading drop and he stiffened all pale, bubbling inside like a teapot. He carried on in the Japanese language, telling some terrible story to himself. At the last he started spilling English: "Five dollars. Five dollars my neighbor offer me for the big piano the day we have to move. Ten years we neighbors and he offer five dollars because he knew we couldn't take but our clothes to the camp. I smash the big piano up instead." He blew a big breath and fell dead quiet. Marie decided he had been talking of trouble he had had with his own house back in the war. She couldn't think what sympathy to give, and Dr. Hastie was at the University, so she hurried through the rest of her work, feeling uneasy about the whole thing.

It didn't make her happier neither to have Buddy Nix waiting at Louise's step for her. He stood fidgeting one foot to the other and picking at his mustache; the Big Man had tied a firecracker to his tail and he was still smoking. "Baby," he said, "they're expecting you at the place Saturday night." Even though they had worked together for three-four years, his face was a stranger's. He had been given his orders, and among his friends, Buddy put himself first.

"That's only two days off," Marie said and shook her head no. He fiddled with the silver money in his pocket. "Maybe I took a little too much expense charge in the past," he mumbled, "but we ought to be able to make a better adjustment from here on."

She shook her head no again. "I'll be back a week from Saturday," she said.

His face stretched a peg, turning from stranger's to enemy's. "You not shopping for a berth with some other establishment? You ought to know that won't do." Marie just walked inside. "A week from Saturday," she said while she slammed the door on him. He looked like a fool-kid, considering the problem on her mind, but she knew he had enough snake in him to add to her stock of worries, all the same.

The morning found things moving smooth and fast, though. She came to work and Dr. Hastie greeted her at the door, waving a deed to a house like it was a pennant at a football game. Behind him Professor Tatsumi stood wearing a smile. She was surprised at his change of mood. Dr. Hastie followed her look and said, "I told him this wasn't wartime, this was peace — so people would listen to reason these days." Marie suspected he was jollying the old man along, but still, the Professor having his peace of mind back was good. When Dr. Hastie asked her to call up Jack and arrange for signing over the deed, she felt real hopeful. She sat easy on the sofa like a real businesswoman and giggled while she heard Jack on the other end of the line struggling to get awake.

She set it up for the two to meet downtown at a notary public's office. Then no sooner had Dr. Hastie left than Jimmy came sneaking in the back door. It was too early for school to be out, and he wasn't even bringing a rat for an excuse. "We got the new house yet?" he asked right off.

"It's on order. But what are you doing around this time of day?" Marie didn't want him getting too close to things. Even though the plan was for his benefit, it could go one way or the other, and neither way might be pretty.

"When do we move in?" he asked.

"Nothing's sure yet."

"I bet that old social-worker woman will drop her uppers when she finds us living in style."

Marie stopped her sweeping to size up Jimmy. He was leaning on the door sill, his eyes cute and shiny, looking at the ceiling and counting the last laughs he would have, like they were flyspecks. She saw he was considering the new house a salvation from his shame of being on probation, all the better because it was located on the spot of his trouble with the law. His gloating was natural enough, but she feared it would sour and spoil him if Louise and Jack didn't move into the house. He might not see how selling it back at a profit would advantage him when it came college time. He might turn to believing that all big ideas were phony. Marie shooed him out to play with the animals in the cages because he was dragging down her mood.

After a while Dr. Hastie returned, pulling Jack inside with him. He told Marie to get some beer from the refrigerator, and they and Professor Tatsumi and Jimmy grouped themselves in the front room. She served like a real hostess, with paper napkins and glasses. Jack squirmed in his chair so bad he couldn't hear the Professor saying what a smart boy Jimmy was.

They had hardly took the foam off the glass when a hard rap-a-tap rattled the front door. Dr. Hastie stretched his neck to peep through the window. "I think it's Martin, the guy I bought the house from," he said in a quiet voice that drowned out all their happy chatter. "He must have got the word even before the ink dried at the notary public's." Marie started up to let this Martin in and Jack excused himself fast to the kitchen. She would have tripped him, if she could have reached, because he was chickening out to leave her do the backing down, in front of Dr. Hastie and Jimmy, if backing down had to be done.

Two men walked in the room. They came in so fast and important-like that she didn't catch a look at them from the front. They stood like buckets of lard, with flat-top panama hats pulled down on their ears and sweat off their fat making their short-sleeve sport shirts sticky wet. They sniffed around the room and then one of them said, "Well, Mister Hastie,

I got to hand it to you. I never thought you college joes had much business sense."

"Thank you, Mister Martin," Dr. Hastie said, without getting out of his chair or offering them one.

"Well, I haven't deposited your check yet. I got it right here," this Martin said and pulled a mailbag-size wallet from his hip and fished around in between twenty-dollar bills and stuff. His buddy watched him with a sour look, like he was a big bulldog waiting to be told to chew everybody up.

It was then that Marie recognized the two of them. It was the way Martin's wattles bunched up under his chin that made her see he was the Big Man — the boss of the bright lights. She had seen him before, counting his money like now, and he had seen her, too, but they hadn't ever talked. The other man was just as bad to be seeing again. A long time back she had had close dealings with him. This time he wasn't wearing his uniform or swinging his blackjack, but he was Sergeant Paefke. Marie shrunk up in her shoes and tried to imagine herself invisible. She heard the argument between the Big Man and Dr. Hastie from a distance, like they were on a radio.

"So what do you say I give your check back and then we can talk about the repairs you want done around here," the Big Man said.

"You're wasting your time. I don't own the house now," Dr. Hastie said.

"Eh? Oh yes, the nigra. Well, goddamn it, tell him to come up to the office and we'll fix his place, too. Boy, wait till the Real Estate Board hears about this stunt. Who'd ever thought of a man's tenants getting together and blackmailing him by buying a house? Well, thank Christ, all my customers ain't college professors."

"I said you were wasting your time. You sold the house,

the deed is signed, the people who own it are going to live there."

The Big Man nodded his head. "Oh yes, oh yes. I suspected as much. You're after a little gravy on the deal. You paid out a thousand. I'll give you two thousand, but not a cent more. All I can say is that you're a hell of a type to be teaching young boys and girls in school."

This was where Marie should have moved in, since she knew what a tough man the Big Man was and now he'd made a profit offer that could end the dispute without blood. But she was too confused. They went talking on, one at the other, hotter and hotter.

"The people are going to live in that house. It's not for sale at any price."

"Then Christ, it's what I though at first. Just plain dumbness. Not smart, just plain dumb. Son, didn't you know that house is in a white neighborhood?"

"It wasn't a white neighborhood a year ago."

"It's a white neighborhood now, professor."

"Who made it a white neighborhood?"

"*I* did. I own the land, I built the houses."

"Well, I bought a house and I decided different. So what right do you have to kick?"

"I hold a quarter-million-dollar investment and you come piss in the stew with your piddling thousand dollars. You don't see the wrong in that?"

"I say if you can be hurt that easy, then you're cheating, Mr. Martin. Your big investment is a phony. It takes more than a horse's ass and some manure to run a livery stable. Now I think you better go."

"You'll see who gets hurt. Half the University's board of trustees are realtors. They are not going to let this kind of thing go on. Not by a damn-sight, they're not."

"I'm willing to make a full-time job of fighting bloodsuckers like you."

Professor Tatsumi stood up then. He made a polite nod to the Big Man and a try at a smile. He said, "Mr. Martin, you smart man or you wouldn't have such business. So what if I make you deal? I try experiment I haven't tried before. If it work you leave things as is. If it don't, then you win."

The Big Man moved close to the Professor, the two of them five-by-five, like a pool ball and a porcelain bowl. The Big Man asked, teasing mean, "What experiment? From the smell in here you must be trying to make perfume out of cow turds."

"It's cats and rats we work with," the Professor started to explain.

"You got *them* back there? That does it. That's all excuse I need for evicting you bastards." The Big Man flapped his stub arms and dug Paefke in the ribs. "My office can handle *that*," he said to him.

Professor Tatsumi gave down, not to the Big Man personal, but more like it was to the bad things a long time back that he had thought was all done. The sight of him made Marie plain mad enough to forget being invisible. She was set to kick the Big Man in the pants, but Dr. Hastie had rose with his fists ready to fight the both of the visitors. Old Paefke reached in his pocket for his blackjack but the Big Man held his arm and headed them for the door. He pushed Paefke outside then stood on the sill. "What, what do you expect to have to show after this is over?" he asked Dr. Hastie and everybody. Then he shut the door easy behind him, not waiting for an answer any more than a toad would if it asked a mosquito how to fly, just before gobbling it up.

"Well, *we*'ll go see the experiment," Dr. Hastie said to the Professor, trying to make light of what had happened. But

Marie could tell from the thinness of his voice that the breaking out of real trouble had shook him. And then Jack came steaming in, shouting at her, "How come he didn't sell? How come? How come?" And Professor Tatsumi answered Dr. Hastie, saying, "Don't bother to come see. The experiment is finish. Jimmy and I take care of it." He took the boy by the shoulder and they headed for the kitchen.

Marie felt split in a dozen parts: Seeing the Big Man and Paefke again, Dr. Hastie shaky, Jack chewing at her, the Professor all broke up, and Jimmy — who she had started the ruckus for and almost forgot about — seeing everything, including the sight of his daddy making a coward of himself. She handled Jack first: "He didn't sell because he didn't want to sell. That don't mean he won't sell when he gets ready."

"I'm quitting this, you hear," Jack said. "This ain't nothing but fool craziness. No part of this is for me."

She got tough. "Okay, Jack, get out tomorrow if you want. But if you want to stay alive tonight you better stick with us now." That put a plug in his mouth. She started nipping at Dr. Hastie's heels: "Jack and I think he and me and Louise better stay here tonight. They won't be so bold in a white-folks neighborhood if they come to bother us. Have you got a gun?" He shook his head no. "Well, Jack's got a bird rifle he'll bring when he comes back with Louise. Jack, you better go now before the sun sets."

It was out of line for her to give orders like that, but Jack jumped and Dr. Hastie took on better color. Marie set off to tend to the Professor and Jimmy next, but when she came on them on the back porch they were stuffing the animals from the cages into gunny sacks, and the Professor gave her such a fierce look that she didn't ask why; she went on back to the front room, stopping on the way to get her and Dr. Hastie fresh beers.

He was turning the pages of the phone book when she sat down by him on the sofa. "How do you call the police?" he asked. She knew what good that would do. "Policemen don't like to come unless there's a body," she told him. "Well, do you know anybody else to call — any Negroes?" he asked. Only one came to her mind — Lawyer Dawkins — but he had died. She shook her head. They sat and sipped their beer. "I know something," he said. "You're putting your own money in this. Why?"

Marie figured that the chances for cash profit had gone flying, so she claimed credit for being virtuous: "It's for Jimmy and his mama Louise. She's been good to me and what's hers is mine." He took her hand when she said that, and she liked his doing it — not so much because it was a white man admiring her. He didn't seem really white right then, just white by accident-like.

And then Louise and Jack came hustling into the house without stopping to knock. Louise had a handkerchief bandage around her forehead, splotched with blood. Dark had set in pretty much outside. Marie jumped up and ran to her sister. "It's just a scratch that won't stop bleeding," Louise said, pushing off help. "I had barely got home and was dusting the front room when a brick came through the window. Some glass slivers hit me. I looked out and saw a big car pull off, so I knew you must have bought the house."

"They went there right from here!" Dr. Hastie shouted.

"Not much was damaged, except the landlord ain't going to like his broken window," Louise said.

Marie laughed. "The landlord broke his own window. The same man owning your place owns this one, and he's the one we bought the house off of."

"Oh? Well, he won't get too rambunctious then." Then Louise had another thought: "But he don't own our new house no more. What's he going to do to *it?*" Marie saw that her sister meant to live in the new house, hell-or-high water.

"It's insured," Dr. Hastie said. "Martin isn't going to risk getting a flock of insurance investigators on his neck."

"Just what this Martin is meaning to do with *us* looks to me the important thing right now," Jack rumbled. "*I'm* insured, too, but that car hanging around outside don't make me feel the better for it."

"That's right, it followed us over," Louise said.

Marie peeked out the window, then smiled to herself at what she saw. There was no mistaking the low yellow shape of the car outside; the man sitting smoking in the driver's seat could only be Buddy Nix, out snooping on her. Maybe he was planning to kidnap her back downtown, the Big Man had thrown such a scare in him. The Big Man's boys were crawling all over, for true. Marie turned to Jack. He had brought his rifle and she took it from him. "Does it make much noise?" she asked. "It's only a .22," he said. "Wait a minute!" Dr. Hastie called out to interfere, but she waved everybody back and pushed the window screen up to open a space.

She kneeled down, took good aim, and fired. "Kaboof!" the white-wall back tire of Buddy's convertible gave out. Buddy just sat there, not knowing what had happened. She cocked the rifle and fired again. This time the front tire exploded and Buddy's car took off like a scalded dog. He must have thrown it into four-five gears at once. The car jumped up, bucked and bounced, then roared and whined along the asphalt, throwing sparks from the rims it rolled on. Marie watched after it until it was out of sight. "Go tell that to the Big Man," she whispered. Then she gave Jack his rifle back and said, "My, ain't it awful, the wrecks that trashy people do drive around."

They stood bug-eyed. Dr. Hastie caught his wits first. He swallowed some beer and said real dry, "I hope you didn't shoot up an innocent party." She told him, "Oh, he wasn't no innocent party. He was a personal friend of mine."

"Where's Jimmy?" Louise asked in sudden worry. Marie led her to the back porch, but there wasn't a sign of him or the Professor. She said they must be out looking for rats, and set Louise to scouting the refrigerator to see what she could make into a supper for the six of them.

Soon there were canned beans, coleslaw and bake potatoes on the table. Jack and Dr. Hastie and Marie and Louise had just set down to them when the missing two showed up. They had stiff, sad faces that made them look alike, the boy and the old man. It was this that stopped Louise when she started to fuss at Jimmy. She began to put food on the plates saved for them. "We got rid of the cats and rats," Professor Tatsumi said dead-like. Dr. Hastie blinked at the news, but didn't say anything.

Even with this — and despite Jack's sulking the whole time, eating with his head almost between his legs — Marie found enjoyment in the meal. She hadn't been equal with her kin for a long time, and with a white man never. Louise was taking some of the same pleasure; regardless of her head hurt she bobbed about like a hummingbird, fetching fresh helpings from the stove.

They were having coffee when the phone rang. Dr. Hastie answered it. From the kitchen they heard him yell "What?" and then tell somebody they couldn't do that, and then cuss and threaten to sue. Marie and the rest went out to the front room. He sat on the sofa jabbing the phone receiver against his leg, his face puddled up with anger. "I told you we had insurance on the house. Now, we *used to* have insurance," he said breathing heavy. "This bird just called to say the policy has been canceled. It wasn't filled out right, he claims. I told him I'd sue, but he just hung up on me."

"So now we know where Martin's going to hit," Marie said. "What are we going to do about it?" Nobody even breathed for a while. Then Louise spoke up: "We got to protect that property. Jack, you and Dr. Hastie are going over there and stop them from what they plan to do."

But Jack dug his heels in. "No! That's hero stuff and I ain't no Hopalong Cassidy. If I went over there it'd be under false pretensions, and there's been enough false pretensions to this already. I thought this was a pure and simple money arrangement but now it looks like the idea is to get us all in jail." He straightened his back and aimed his long jaw at Dr. Hastie. "You meant for us to live in that house?" he accused. "Why did you want us to, when you didn't even know us? Was it just because we was colored, and that any colored persons would have suited as good? I don't see where being considered just any colored man makes me obliged to you in this. You might have intended good, but I wasn't considered in any personal fashion, so I don't feel no personal connection."

Before his remarks could set off any hoo-raw Marie said quick, "Okay, Jack, me and Dr. Hastie will go to the house. It'd be better for you to stay here and watch after Louise, anyway. Give me your rifle."

But Louise wasn't for letting her husband off the hook. "Wait a minute," she said. "You bawl this white man out for treating you like a black nothing when he offers you a chance to be a something. But you *are* a black nothing until you do something and be something. You been a black nothing all your life to every white man, and if you think the way you do, you're going to be nothing to me, from now on, too. *I'll* keep watch on our house."

Jack was stung and begged no, no, and Marie joined in to persuade Louise not to. Marie told her it wasn't smart for them all to be in one place, because Martin might send a gang to wreck all three houses. Jimmy and Professor Tatsumi could stay here and Louise and Jack could go back to their old house and stand guard there. Jack agreed quick to that, but Louise brushed him away with a scorning look. "I'll stay *here.* I want to be in earshot of any rumpus that happens at our new house, and if something happens I'll call the police, the fire department and the charity hospital to pick up what's left of them and me, because I'm going to run over there soon as I put the phone down. I'll stay here, that is, on one condition. Jack, you're going to tell Marie and Dr. Hastie that you would go out there with them if you didn't have to stay and protect me. Now tell them that."

"I have to stay with Louise," Jack said like she ordered, his face painful. Dr. Hastie hadn't taken offense. He put his hand on Jack's shoulder, smiled, and started to speak, but then shrugged off the words.

"*I* want to be a scout. I'll take messages back and forth and keep a lookout," Jimmy piped in. "I don't want to sit and wait when there's nothing going to happen here, you said yourself."

Marie laughed at this grown-man boldness, but she couldn't see putting the seed corn in the grinder. Besides, Professor Tatsumi was standing off in a fog and needed watching over. "No, you and the Professor will have to go over to your mama and papa's and take care of the belongings there." Her look told him how bad the old man was feeling and Jimmy scraped his feet and agreed to the nurse job.

Marie picked up the rifle in the corner by the window. "How many bullets you got?" she asked. Jack fished his pocket and came up with four. She took them and joked to

Dr. Hastie, "There's two to fight with and one apiece to blow our brains out with." And the two of them went off to the new house like to a picnic.

It was about nine o'clock when they reached the Big Man's row of little blue houses, each of them about twenty feet away from one another. People were living in some and others were empty. Even though the moon shone bright, Dr. Hastie had to strike a match and read the tag on the keys to be sure which was theirs. They found it near the end of the line. The house on one side was occupied, that on the other side didn't have a roof on it yet.

"If you look at it one way, this is a hell of a thing to be fighting for," he said. "You'd think people would be fighting to get out of these installment-plan whore-cribs."

The inside of the house stood bare. The hardwood floor shone pale yellow where the light from the outside came through the windows. Patches of sawdust made splotches on it. Dr. Hastie flicked the light switch without thinking that the power hadn't been turned on yet. "We should have brought candles," Marie said. They peeked in the rooms — the front room, kitchen and the two bedrooms were laid out like leaves of a four-leaf clover, with a little stem for the toilet. They decided she should stay in the kitchen and watch the back while he minded the front. But after a while he called her in with him. "Come watch our neighbor's television set," he said. "I don't know which is the worst punishment — this hard floor, or seeing those poor bastards over there hypnotized to their easy chairs by that big glass eye. Besides, if anyone comes they'll probably drive up along the road out here."

Out the window that opened on the carport she could see through the bedroom window of the next house right to the television set standing in the living room. The room was shadowy but she could make out from the blue light of the screen a child on the floor and, sitting on each side of the door frame, a man and a woman. The scene looked so peaceful it drove home to Marie how wild a thing she was doing now. She thought back to the bragging she and Alexander had done right after the trouble with Sergeant Paefke. Well, she was on White Folks' Avenue, all right, but it was a black, empty house. She had spent all her money and still wasn't even with Paefke or anybody. By whatever count she was worse off than she had been years back — she couldn't even count on being a whore any more.

Dr. Hastie was squatting in the middle of the room so he could watch both the window to next door and the window to the street. She sat down beside him and leaned her elbows on her knees and her head on her hands so he couldn't see her face. "Pillows and whiskey are what we need, pillows and whiskey and tobacco," he complained. "But no, we just flew off like a couple of wild geese."

"We sure took off, all right," she said, all choked up.

Just then there was a scurrying of little feet in the front bedroom. He jumped up to investigate, holding the rifle ready. "A rat," he said when he looked inside. "A rat already. That's funny in such a new building." He came back and sat down and talked on. "I guess we're the pioneer type. We come to clear the wilderness with our rifle so the settlers can move in with their television aerials. That's progress. Except if we manage to hang on to this house, and Louise and Jack get to live like everybody else, I'd like to hope they won't *be* like everybody else. Tatsumi's cats and rats learned to get along, but they kept their souls and their taste buds."

"Negroes are just people," Marie said, with her lips in between her teeth to hold back from crying out loud.

He took that for a smart saying and laughed. "Yes, that's

the whole point. I guess you tricked Jack into this, same as you tricked me. He didn't want to be pushed around when he saw what it was. He didn't want to be prodded out of being one of the herd, that is. Louise now, she's ready to fight — but isn't this matchbox house all she's fighting for? So that leaves only you holding the bag with the big idea in it. And I want to know, are you a freak, just like I'm a freak white man?"

She realized his chatter had been because he wasn't feeling much better than she was. "You're forgetting Jimmy," she said, trying to think hopeful. "His folks can't go but so far in the years they've got left. He's starting out, and this house here might start him off good."

Before he could answer they heard Jimmy himself outside, calling in a big whisper, "Auntie Marie, Auntie Marie." She went to the window. "What are you doing out there?" she asked, trying to sound mad.

"Oh there you are," he answered, standing like a little splinter in the broad moonlight. "I came to see how things was. I tried three-four places before finding this one."

"Things are fine. You get on back home now," she ordered.

He stalled, looking up at the roof and around. "So this is ours. I wish I'd known it was before."

"What do you mean?" Marie asked. Jimmy was on the sidewalk, but the front lawn was so narrow she could talk to him from out the window without too much risk of rousting the neighbors.

"Well, the Professor and I went out delivering the rats this afternoon — "

"I thought you chloroformed them," Dr. Hastie said, joining Marie at the window.

"No sir. He started to, but then he thought we might as

well make presents of them. We put them out one and two a time all along here. But if we'd known this was the house, we'd have skipped this one."

Dr. Hastie held back laughing long enough to ask, "What about the cats, what did you do with them?"

"We let them off at the same places."

Dr. Hastie bent over. "Oh God, what a business. They give them the rats and then furnish cats that won't catch them. That Tatsumi, that Tatsumi."

Marie held a straight face so she could chase Jimmy away, but when he had gone the comedy didn't seem so funny. "What about Professor Tatsumi?" she asked. "We ruined the experiment he set a great store in."

"Yes, yes, we did," Dr. Hastie said. "But he wasn't really building anything, he was sifting the ruins of what had been done to him years ago."

"I thought it was a pretty good idea."

"Mr. Martin, the real estate man, didn't."

"You're being hard on your friend," Marie blamed him and they sat quiet a while before he said, "I'm being hard to keep from being scared." His expression was so clear and bright that she slid over without thinking and caught him around the waist and pushed him backward to the floor. She crawled on his body like it was a log in a stormy sea, until she looked down into his eyes. His eyes were wide, where they had opened in surprise, but the surprise had gone and they showed cool calm. She feared his mouth and its dimples would roll up with disgust.

Instead, with the calmness still on his face he reached his hands about her shoulders and wrapped her in, taking her but not pulling at her. His move was easy, like he had had her before and knew he was to have her again — a wife-love move. She kissed him. He was the first white man she had ever kissed on the lips.

In the long kiss Marie got so close to Dr. Hastie she could see how far apart they were. He liked her and respected her because she had done a deed it took courage for a Negro to do. He had high respect for the Negro people and wanted them to act with courage. He was in love with courage because he wasn't sure he had it himself. She knew he did, though — not from his buying the house or his brave show against the Big Man, but right then, from how he handled her. There is a way in man-woman sex to tell courage or cowardness. She knew she might be able to persuade him he had courage, but that didn't mean she should mix in with his deep emotions, even if she had been white as an angel outside and in. He had ideas and guts that needed to be put other places than in the fight that being with her would mean. She rolled free of him. "I'm sorry, I was scared," she said.

He straightened up and said, "You know, now that I'm practically an ex-employee of the University I was thinking about heading for Canada. And in Canada, you know — " He didn't have chance for more words. Like somebody was trying to throw cold water on his thoughts, a splash of liquid came through the open window to the front and hit the floor, splattering on them. It was a surprising thing, and before they moved, a second splash landed. "Gasoline!" Dr. Hastie shouted and they scrambled to the window, him grabbing the rifle off the floor.

Outside, a man was walking with his back to them toward a car. He had a bucket in each hand and went along so slow and casual he could have been a farmer carrying milk. Another man sat in the open front doorway of the car, holding a bundle of rags and trying to set it afire with matches. The two of them were dressed alike, with fancy sport shirts and panama hats. They didn't suspect anybody was in the house.

"Shoot them. Shoot one and they'll run," Marie whispered to Dr. Hastie. They were in easy target distance. But instead, he leaned out the window and called, "You guys there! Get away from here. Get away from this property." The one with the buckets turned around and the other stood up in the road. "It must be the jerk that bought the house, the professor," the one with the buckets said. "Yeah, he'd better get out of there," the other said, and he yelled back to Dr. Hastie in a sarcastic voice, "You're in our way, prof. Go on home and grade papers. We got a job to do."

Dr. Hastie poked the rifle out. "I've got a gun," he warned. "He's got a gun, Catlett," the man with the buckets said to his buddy. "It looks more like a fountain pen to me, Dago," the one called Catlett answered and they just stood there. "Shoot one of the bastards, shoot one," Marie begged Dr. Hastie. He pulled the trigger, but he aimed the bullet over their heads. The two out there, Catlett and Dago, moved then. They ran around to the far side of their car, pushing each other and skidding on the gravel as they went. They scrunched down behind the engine hood. Catlett stuck his arm up and waved a big pistol. "We got guns, too. Real guns. So give up, fellow. We don't want no muss." His voice wasn't kidding this time.

"Damn this rifle! It doesn't make enough noise," Dr. Hastie fussed. "We'll never attract any help, unless they start shooting." "If they start shooting we won't need help. Help won't do no good," Marie told him. The gasoline vapors spread thick in the room, making a raw dangerous smell. The men outside were talking to each other, but too low for their words to be understood. They scraped the buckets around on the road gravel, and then a blue flame puffed up, showing they had started a fire in one of them. The bucket came flying through the air and crashed against the window sill, just missing coming inside the house; the man who flung it had aimed a little too low. The burning rags that were in it spilled out and lay sizzling on the lawn. Dr. Hastie fired the rifle wild in surprise. The two men cussed and started to work on the other bucket.

Dr. Hastie fired again, low this time, trying to hit them by shooting underneath the car, but the bullet bounced off a wheel. He had only one shot left. He turned to Marie: "Go run to the house next door and ask them to call the police." But instead, she grabbed the rifle from his hands. "There ain't time and you going to need me here," she said, and she went to the window facing the house next door. She pointed the rifle out, aiming right at the lighted television screen in the middle of the family group. She didn't care about the risk, she fired, and Pouf! the screen churned out white smoke and went black. The man watcher jumped from his chair and ran to the door.

Just then the second bucket hit the window right in front of Dr. Hastie. He stuck out his hands to bat it away, but the bottom caught him on the jaw and knocked him to the floor. The burning rags dropped on his chest and stuck there like a crazy necktie. Marie brushed them off with a sweep of her hands. Almost before they hit the floor, the room seemed to heave and belch, and everything became flames.

Marie was able to drag Dr. Hastie out the front door, somehow. She got him to the lawn and kneeled over him. Her eyes stung too bad to see, so she could only slap like crazy all over his body where she thought clothes might be burning, and at her own body where it hurt. She heard the man from next door yelling at the two men's car driving off. She heard the house crackling as the fire took hold. She stopped slapping and rubbed her eyes to try to be able to see something. The first thing she saw was Dr. Hastie's body. Black-looking blood trickled out the side of his mouth and a ragged black-rim circle showed where the fire had burned through his shirt. Even in the moonlight the flesh of his chest showed how meat-raw it was. But he was still breathing, breathing almost natural, and his face still had the round look of hope of a baby rooster. She brushed a piece of smut off his nose and thought of the scars he would carry from this. She had given him something to remember her by. Maybe he would take them as medals to prove to himself he had courage.

Marie sat there in a mixed-up, dog-tired way, not feeling pain or thinking straight, when Louise came running up. Louise shook her shoulder and Marie said she and Dr. Hastie weren't too bad off. Louise looked from them to the fire. "They did it, they did it," she moaned. But then her anger rose and she shook a finger at the flames. "Did you see them? Would you know them if you saw them again?" Marie had almost forgot there was a house. She looked up and saw it was almost gone. Off to the side she saw that the man from next door had hitched up his garden hose and was sprinkling the ground to make sure the fire wouldn't spread to his home. Him standing there set her to laughing so hard she would have fallen over if Louise hadn't held her. "Do you remember them?" Louise kept asking. "The police will be here and you can tell them. They will have to do something about something this bad."

Thought of police stopped Marie's laughing. The two men who burned the house were probably two patrolmen Paefke had sent. Everybody belonged to the Big Man. The police, the land — her. She knew it was time to plan to travel. She got on her feet just when Jimmy, Jack and Professor Tatsumi galloped up, one behind the other, all bug-eyed with worry. She talked to them fast. She told Jack to help Louise carry Dr. Hastie home and to get Jimmy away from there before he had his probation taken away. She told Professor

Tatsumi: "This is all because of your idea and you ought to feel good. It worked, it worked with the people, if not with the house." And to Jimmy she said, "I'm going on a trip now, but once your mama writes me you're doing poor in school I'll be back and beat on you, you hear?" She had only one more thing on her mind. She pointed to Dr. Hastie. "If he asks about me, let him know all there is, everything." The truth couldn't hurt her with him, he had her souvenir on his chest.

Marie made a good goodbye of it. The menfolk listened with their heads down. But Louise just shook out her apron like it was a battleflag and kneeled by Dr. Hastie. "*He'll* remember what they looked like and we'll get them," she promised, while Marie went her way into the night.

The Woman finished telling her story with her eyes fixed on Sam, like she was talking just to him. He could not read her expression, whether she was bragging over the deed she had done or was flaunting the white professor she had had for friend. It could have been she figured he was the only one listening. The rocking boxcar and the heat of afternoon had clabbered up the whiskey inside the rest. Good-Rocking Poppa was resting his head in one hand in sleep-thought and the Spook lay stretched out on his belly. Only Shorty and Teacher-Man sat up straight but it wouldn't do to blow on them too hard. The Woman waited for somebody to say something, then grabbed the moonshine jar from Teacher-Man's hands in scorning fashion and took a big drink. Sam squeezed his brains for words, but nothing came.

She climbed to her feet and wobbled to the end of the car,

off by herself with her back turned. Sam tested to himself some story beginnings that would make his life's doings sound big and brave, to show her she wasn't all that much. Then he heard her crying, shaking and choking, her head bent down ashamed-like. He saw that maybe she hadn't been meaning to boast but had wanted kind words. He decided to go over and talk. "Where you heading now?" he asked to be asking. "I'm going to borrow a cup of sugar to make pancakes," she said hoarse and bitter-like, keeping her back to him. He didn't want to be teased at and he started to move away. She turned around and spoke more friendly, smiling some though her eyes were puffy. "No," she said, "I ain't got nothing cooking. I'm just an easy rider. Like the song goes, 'Easy rider, won't be back till fall — But if I find me a good man, I won't be back at all.' " She made a sassy twitch of her hips but she looked at him steady and he felt itchy and sweaty something awful.

A nasty smell sprung up, cutting through the dust-and-whiskey odor of the boxcar. Good-Rocking Poppa woke and spit and looked around. "Chrissakes, who did that?" he asked. "That's a paper-mill stink. We must be getting near a big town," Shorty answered him. "Birmingham?" Poppa guessed, and everyone stirred at the word. The Spook rolled off his belly and moved out of sight from the open door. The others scooched back too but peeked out.

The land was rolling now almost without letup, and so red was the clay on the ground that the path cut for train track looked like it had been sliced from the backs of big whales. Neither trees nor grass amounted to much — except they passed close to a long pecan orchard laid out in razor-straight rows, where fat milk cows looked to be leaning against the tree trunks while they munched their fill in the shade of lazy green leaves that kept all sun glare out. It made Sam close his eyes and try to die for longing.

Then they saw the paper mill with its tall chimney smoking, off where the highway went by. The train took a sharp turn and they were in the city. The lumberyard and grain supply and wholesale part of the city, anyway. There were old brick and sheet-metal places with cobblestone streets in front, and even before the train passed the brown-trimmed yellow station with a sign saying TUSCALOOSA on it, Sam knew it wasn't Birmingham. They went right through and did another curve to leave that city behind. Everybody sort of stretched themselves in thanks that the train did not stop.

And then the train did stop. It slowed and shuddered and jerked to a halt out in the middle of nowhere. Right at once the boxcar seemed to pump steam. It was hot before, but without the little breeze it blew by moving, it was hell-hot. "We ain't going to start backwards now, are we?" Teacher-Man asked all worried. Nobody gave answer. The time stretched by. "Look see if the engine might have pulled off," Poppa asked for somebody to stick their neck out. "I see the smoke pass. It's still here," Shorty said. Sam slid on his bottom to the closed door, figuring to open it and make a draft — but Poppa hauled him short by ordering, "Unh-uh, buddy. That'd make too much light on us." Sam slid over to the open door then, to catch some air, and down the embankment in a big hollow he saw a sight that glittered his eyes. Somebody had dug out a big pond, a fishing lake, down there. It was as clear as a mirror glass and a barber couldn't have trimmed its bank in neater style. Some shade trees with benches under them stood by the pond, and a rowboat, ready to go, lay in the water, its nose to the bank. No people were down there; if you judged from looks, any man — white or black — was welcome to wash away his cares. Sam couldn't help saying "Goddamn, goddamn" out loud. The others pushed close, frightened at first, then they let their eyes feast.

"I think I'll take me a little swim while we wait for this

airplane to gas up," the Spook said and started to jump out. But Poppa held him by the collar. "You'll be swimming in your own teeth and blood if you try," he warned rough. "Don't you know the trainmen are likely walking round out there, stretching their legs? They'll see you for sure, and they'll find the rest of us." More than one pair of hands were ready to grab the Spook when Poppa presented that idea, and he slipped back to the middle of the car, ashamed at being shamed. Nobody paid him more attention, but looked on at the pond, leaning forward like they were trying to cast their reflections in the water.

The Woman was standing behind the row of men and she put her hands on Sam's shoulders and leaned down on him while he squatted. It was all right having her body close, but his belt buckle jammed into his belly fierce and he was obliged to straighten his back. She seemed to mistake his moving and she pulled back and kicked him sharp in the rump. He didn't even grunt, not wanting the others to notice. He thought of trying to explain to her he hadn't been shaking her off, but feared that would sound foolish. He kept on looking at the pond.

The Spook spoke up from where he was lying on his back. He sounded so cheery and at ease that he drew all eyes. "Too hot for whiskey, too risky to swim, so I'm going to take the smoke that never fails to drown trouble," he said, and he waved a cigarette which was homemade out of wrapping paper and burned with the smell of rotten rags. "It's my last one, but I'm offering drags to any who wants to join me on the moon."

"A tea-sniffer! I could've guessed," Poppa said and spit on the floor. The Woman raised her eyebrows then drifted off to the side to fiddle with her hair. But the three country men — Shorty, Teacher-Man and Sam — had never seen that kind of thing before, and the Spook was willing to put on a show. He held that cigarette with both hands, sucked hard and loud on it, then stuck his hand over his mouth to keep the smoke in, and began swallowing up and down, his throat muscles moving his Adam's apple around like a snake eating an egg. His eyelids were closed but they could hardly hold in his eyes when they started bugging for air after some seconds passed. "Man, somebody stop that smoke from leaking out his ears," Shorty said in joke, but it looked like a mean hocus-pocus to be doing for fun, and nobody laughed. The Spook finally let the smoke out, and he grinned and panted and offered the cigarette for somebody else to take. "You got to get that cool smoke down into your stomach for the effect," he said.

Teacher-Man showed the most curiosity, but he finally shied off: "I understand if you start using them things you can't never stop." The Spook coughed some before he answered, "Oh no, man, you're talking about coke or snow; these roaches are just a cheap drunk and you don't get no hangover neither. They're easier on you than tobacco. They're just like sex. A man takes what he can get and much as he can stand, but when he's through, he's through." He puffed again, this time not holding the smoke in quite as long as before. In the middle of his third try it looked like a rubber band had snapped in his backbone. He jerked in little ripples all along his body, then lay soft as wax on the floor, smiling lazy-like at the roof of the car.

"Of course," the Spook said, "old marijuana can do some funny things. A friend of mine had a real wild time because he happened to breathe in an overdose. He did everything but twist the devil's tail." And then, while his hand sort of floated the cigarette back and forth from his mouth, he told all about his friend's adventure.

The Spook's Story

THIS FELLOW Willie Jordan held down two jobs in earning his living. He worked at a bank and at a newspaper. He really cleaned up — with a rag and a broom, and ran errands to boot. But those two big jobs weren't enough to keep him out of trouble. He had two wives and two sets of kids to go with the jobs — and a girl friend to hide out with when both wives started picking on him at once. This Willie was a numerous character.

The particular day all hell busted loose started when he was walking between jobs, from the bank to the newspaper. He worked from three in the morning to noon for the bank, polishing and sweeping and doing chores, and then from twelve-thirty to nine at night at the newspaper office, polishing and sweeping and doing chores. The paper was a morning paper, and so none of the editors and reporters came to work much before two in the afternoon.

In his half hour of free time between brooms it was Willie's custom to smoke his lunch in an alleyway. He'd take just half a roach, only enough to make him feel a new day was starting, no more no less. But that day, not only were his two wives mad at him but his girl friend had told him not to come back until he was ready to say he'd marry her. Thinking on these problems made him go past the limit on his butt. When he got up and walking, he thought he was making giant steps on the pavement. But when he closed one eye to squint at the clock on the newspaper office outside wall, he was fifteen minutes late for work.

There wouldn't have been much mind paid even if he had been later, except for the managing editor, Mr. Kaplin, and his ashtray. A managing editor is the man right next to the top man, The Editor. His job is to keep everybody working hard as they can but making sure they don't claim overtime pay for it. Mr. Kaplin had a little glassed-in cubbyhole to himself on the side of the newsroom. He had a big glass-top desk, too, but he didn't get to spend much time at it, because his duty kept him wandering around to spy out loafers. Maybe it was because of this that he set so much store in the horseshoe-shape gold-color ashtray which sat on his desk even though he didn't smoke. He came in every day at one o'clock, ahead of the others so he could tell if they were late, and he wanted that ashtray polished and waiting for him. Even if no visitor had used the tray the day before, Mr. Kaplin would know if Willie hadn't polished it and would bless him out for not doing his orders. Mr. Kaplin was a Jewish fellow and The Editor and the owners and most of the workers weren't, so Willie figured the ashtray was the thing in his mind that kept his desk nailed down so the bosses wouldn't push him back to being a proofreader, or so the smart-aleck city editor wouldn't shove past him.

When Willie came in walking on marshmallows he went straight into Mr. Kaplin's office to get the job done, but the managing editor was there already. Willie hung his head, ready for his beating.

"I see you missed the boat again," said Mr. Kaplin, his puny body stiff like a toothpick, its upper half stuck as high above the top of the desk as it could reach. "Why can't you remember such a simple thing as cleaning up my desk?" He had a real hard point, because somebody had left a cigarette butt squished right in the middle of the gold horseshoe.

Willie shuffled his feet to brace himself for the chewing

out. But then, like a bubble out of dishwater, a second head popped up on Willie's shoulders, another head with eyes and nose and everything. It puffed into being quick as a blister, but with no pain or strain. Willie's rightful head peered over at it, but it paid him no mind. This Second Head looked like Willie, but its chin stuck out and its eyebrows grooved, and it pointed at Mr. Kaplin man-to-man. "I was delayed on personal business," it said, asking nobody's by-your-leave. "I got personal problems like anybody else. I planned to clean your place up now. You should give me credit for good intentions, the way you would anyone else."

Willie's Old Head sneaked a fearful look at Mr. Kaplin, expecting the double-dip worst now. But Mr. Kaplin instead took a moony expression on his bald bony face, his eyes behind his glasses going blank and his little mouth turning button-round. "Well, I guess so," he said.

But the Second Head wouldn't let good enough alone. "You know, Mr. Kaplin," it said, "a man gets mighty tired of cleaning out ashtrays. He has the problems any man has, but what does he have to fight them with — a rag and a broom. Which wouldn't be so bad maybe, if he knew he had a chance for something different. But no, it's a rag and a broom for all of his life, no matter what he does."

Whether the managing editor was startled sidewise or whether he thought how he was a Jew fellow and for the same reasons as Willie he wasn't ever going to move farther along in the newspaper, he anyways nodded his head up and down to agree. "It's bad, all right," he said. "The best you can do is hope it won't be as tough for your kids when, God help them, they have to set out in the world. Do you have any kids, Willie?"

The Second Head gave an unbelieving smile and shrugged Willie's shoulders. It wouldn't even answer the question.

Willie's Old Head spoke up to keep from seeming sassy: "I've got four, sir." Then before he could make any more remarks to get things back to normal, the Second Head pulled him right out of the office — not letting him clean the ashtray.

Willie felt he had to go to the bathroom. He walked past the rows of desks and typewriters in the newsroom to the hallway. From force of habit he started up the stairs to the composing room where there was a toilet in a little closet he always used. There was a toilet in the hall outside the newsroom, too, a big place with hand basins and mirrors, but he knew better than use it, even if there wasn't a WHITE MEN ONLY sign on its frosted glass door. That Second Head, though, didn't have good sense. It turned him away from the stairs and pushed him right through the door to the white men's room.

Willie didn't see anybody in there, and so he started doing his business at one of the standing-up urinals with an easy mind. But from one of the shuttered toilets somebody stepped out and said Hello. Both of his heads peeked back and saw Don Pounds, the sports editor. Willie couldn't tell the spirit of his greeting, but he could guess why Pounds was at the office early. He probably hadn't gone home from work last night and was just now putting himself together for another day's work. Daylight Don, they called him, because he was a real drinking man. He handled himself and his whiskey in neat style. Only the wrinkles and the zigzag red dashes on his pale face gave him away; for the rest he stood slim and trim, with dignified gray touches in his black hair. "How are you, Mr. Don," Willie's Old Head said and started studying his action at the urinal real close. But the Second Head watched the sports editor hitch up his pants and wash his hands and face in the basin. "When are they going to let

Negroes play ball in the Southern League, Mr. Don?" it asked and Willie almost urinated all over the wall. "You fool," his Old Head cursed, "you're bound and determined to force trouble."

Mr. Don stuck a red-rim eye out of the basin. "I expect it'll be soon," he said. "Nobody's going to the games any more. They'll have to do something to improve the crowds, or close down the ball park. God knows, if they can get a grandstand full of Negroes cheering at a Negro getting a chance to play, at least they are giving somebody something to cheer about. Otherwise, the team is just nine guys named Joe and the fans are home drinking beer in front of their TV sets." He went back to splashing the cobwebs off his face.

Willie's Second Head chewed on this a bit, then it asked, "What about the newspapers? Do you think they'd get more readers if they gave the Negro more attention?" Mr. Don straightened up on that. He could have been mad or it might have been soap in his eyes. Willie didn't wait to learn; he buttoned his fly and left fast.

The afternoon's work was usual enough. Willie went around passing a rag over the tops of the reporters' desks and dumping waste baskets into a canvas-sided wagon he pushed along. His Old Head felt ordinary and he had nothing on his mind except for a dull spot where the Second Head was laying dozing, bored with the job. The reporters came in one after another and he gave most of them greetings. Don Pounds was sitting in the corner group of desks that was the sports department, studying the Racing Form. Willie kept away from that part of the newsroom, saving it till the last in hopes Mr. Don would have gone out by then. But finally he had to work by there. He bent way low and polished the desks on tiptoes. The sports editor saw him and spoke all the same. "Willie," he called. "Oh Willie."

"You answer him, you son of a bitch, you started all this,"

Willie's Old Head jostled the Second Head. But the Second Head was having a faraway dream of its own and wouldn't be bothered. The Old Head had to answer Yessir real polite.

"You said something in the washroom about the newspaper giving the Negro a better break," Mr. Don said. "What did you have in mind?" Willie only had in mind a great nervousness about what Mr. Don had in mind and couldn't speak. But of course the Second Head woke up and made ready to stick its nose in. "Well, I tell you what I thought of," Mr. Don went on. "I thought we might add a column of Negro sports news to the sports page."

"That's a good idea — if you do it right," the Second Head declared.

Mr. Don agreed easy enough. "It'd have to be done right. A Negro would do the writing, and he'd have to be damn good."

"You couldn't just limit him to writing about Negro events neither. He'd have to be let free to talk about things in general, or he couldn't keep any self-respect," the Second Head advised in its bold style.

"You know anybody who'd be able to do it?" Mr. Don asked. Willie's Old Head and his Second Head looked at each other. They didn't know anybody. And then Pouf! a third head popped up right between them two. Willie felt dizzy, like he was turning into a vase for somebody to stick flowers in. This Third Head, cool and careful with its words, started talking and smiling with Mr. Don, smooth as syrup. "Why, if you were planning such a thing I'd be a fool not to ask the chance," it said. "I haven't much formal schooling, but I've been around and I've kept my eyes open."

Mr. Don gave a half smile like he'd known all the time Willie would offer himself and he told Willie to sit down at a typewriter and do a sample of his writing. "We'll have to wrangle with old Kaplin about a deal big as this, so I want some ammunition for when we go in his office," he said.

Willie couldn't see to the end of his nose — or noses — where all this was going. He hadn't done more than fun around with a typewriter at odd times when nobody was in the newsroom. But what struck him hardest from the start was just sitting down at the desk. White people wouldn't notice a hundred Negro people if they were walking around with brooms in their hands. Let one sit down and look like he is doing some thinking and every eye turns to him. The newsroom was filled and busy now, and if Willie had had an alarm clock in his pants he couldn't have got more attention. His Old Head looked off to one side, trying to show he didn't mean too serious what he was doing; the Second Head pointed the other way, sneering at all the reporters for being nosy.

One fancy-dressed woman, a society-page writer, spilled some papers on the floor on purpose and started squawking for him to come pick up the mess. The Second Head locked eyes with her and told her bold: "Just a minute. I only got two hands."

But his Third Head didn't pay mind to none of this. It licked its lips and pecked out a steady string of words, words remembered from headlines in the paper and from what it had heard said, and even some words of its own. At the end of a half hour or so, two pages were finished and Willie shoved them to Mr. Don, who was still studying his racing paper. He took out a long black pencil and started stroking and making marks, at almost every letter, it seemed. It looked bad. But when he got to the end he nodded his head and said, "Okay, okay. Now let's go see Kaplin about demoting you from the broom brigade to the sports department."

Walking behind Mr. Don, Willie and his three heads started giggling and laughing to themselves. He began figuring how he would settle with his wives and girl friend so that he could live all new, with no woman on his mind instead of three. And no more lunching off reefers, neither; this fresh start would be meat and potatoes, white shirt, and straight and narrow.

Mr. Kaplin sank deep in himself while he heard the plan, like he was trying to play turtle with his desk for a shell. Mr. Don, standing in front of him, put the pressure on, saying it would be good for circulation and that being the first to do it would get the newspaper a lot of national praise and attention. Willie and his Third Head, standing beside the sports editor, put on a bright smile; the Old Head and the Second Head pulling back to let the other handle this. "I agree that the proposition has some good points, but there are lots of angles to be looked into," Kaplin finally said. He turned in his swivel chair and frowned at the window. Then he took off his glasses and looked back at the two of them in a fuzzy way, like he had put a lace curtain between him and them. Taking off his glasses seemed to have unbuttoned his face, too. His eye sockets showed deep and tired blue, and little dough cookies lumped on his cheeks and around his snubbed-off nose. "I'm going to have to ask some mighty personal questions," he said.

Willie's Third Head looked agreeable and ready.

"To start, how many years school do you have?"

"I went through the eighth grade, sir."

"Only the eighth grade, eh," the managing editor repeated, but Mr. Don defended Willie: "Hell, I never got farther than the seventh, myself. Besides, he writes pretty fair for a rookie."

"Are you married?"

"Yessir."

"Any children?"

"Yessir." Willie remembered telling Mr. Kaplin this only

a few hours before. He got the funny feeling he was talking to a different man.

"Are you married legal?"

At this question Willie's Second Head cocked an eye and snorted through its nose, but the Old Head signaled for it to keep quiet. Mr. Don fidgeted, too, and Willie hoped he'd say something, but he didn't. "Not exactly," the Third Head finally admitted, looking down at the reflection of its scared eyes on the glass-top desk.

Mr. Kaplin gave no sign of hearing the answer. "Have you ever been arrested?" he asked. Willie knew then that this was getting rough. His Third Head fell silent and his Old Head had to answer Yessir. Mr. Don was stirred to complain: "For Chrissakes, Kaplin, you're not hiring a choirboy! I'll match my jail record with anybody's. And what about that New Year's Eve when you were out — "

The managing editor didn't wiggle a muscle of pity. He raised his voice until it rattled hollow on the glass walls of the office. His lips stayed stiff and he didn't seem to be talking to either Mr. Don or Willie: "I've got to know. I've got to know these things. That's what I'm paid for. So let's go on. Do you have a venereal disease? Clap? Siph?"

Willie's three heads were all confused among themselves. One wanted to spit, one wanted to run, one wanted to cry. It was then that a Fourth Head popped up, pushing the others to the side and bouncing them like punching bags. This Fourth Head was red as a penny and twice as hard. "No!" it shouted into the face of Mr. Kaplin, but the word seemed to bounce off the lace curtain he had drawn up in front of him.

"How many times a week do you take a bath?" Mr. Kaplin asked again in his same big hollow voice. But even he knew that was too raw to deserve answer and he went on without waiting for one: "You understand that your background is different from that of the rest of our employees, so if we hired you, *if* we hired you, you couldn't have your friends coming to visit you at the office or anything like that."

"None of my friends would feel it an honor to mingle around here," the Fourth Head said. Willie's other heads knew trouble was sure to come soon if this kept on. They looked to Mr. Don for rescue, but he had backed off and was watching glass-eyed.

"In fact," Mr. Kaplin said, "you probably couldn't work in the newsroom at all. We'd have to find you a place off to the side somewhere, or else there'd be talk."

"How about that little toilet up in the composing room?" the Fourth Head asked hot and sarcastic. "It wouldn't be noticed any more than your office and it wouldn't smell as bad."

That remark stirred up Mr. Kaplin, but in a funny way. His face split into a razor smile and he nodded, saying, "Exactly. You're at least a Negro now, but if you start wearing a tie to work here, you might as well be a — "*Jew* was the word he said to end with, but before he spoke it, Willie's Fourth Head, fierce as fire, picked up the gold-color horseshoe ashtray and slammed it down on the glass-top desk.

The glass didn't even chip. But the ashtray divided into a dozen chunks and just lay broken on top of the desk. The plop it made popped all Willie's extra heads and left him by himself. He could only think to run. But like a goodbye shot from one of the vanished heads, he found himself shouting, "I'll be back one day, you bastard!" And then he ran.

Neither Mr. Kaplin or Mr. Don made a move after him. Mr. Kaplin only called out, "Bring some more along with you when you come." And then he started laughing or crying, one or the other. Willie didn't look back to see which. All this wild experience sent him sailing down the stairs and out to the sidewalk. A white folks' taxicab was sitting out in front of the building with the motor running, but nobody in it, not even a driver, and Willie jumped behind the steering wheel and took off.

When Willie woke up he smiled to himself before he opened his eyes because he knew he had been having a bad dream. He tried to guess where he was lying. His girl friend's bed, he decided, and he straightened up to see if he was right. He banged his head so hard on the bottom of the taxi meter box that it sent him back down again. He eased his eyes around and saw himself on the front seat of the taxi he remembered having driven off. He crawled to a sitting up position. He was out near a dock on the river front. Somehow the taxi's front fenders had gotten curled back and wrapped around the headlights. Willie decided he'd get out and take a walk — a long walk right out of town.

The Spook finished his story about the same time he finished his reefer cigarette. He didn't smoke it to a stump and quit, he balanced it on his thumbnail and sucked it to the last wisp, even swallowing sparks.

"Which do you think that Mr. Kaplin was doing, laughing or crying?" Shorty asked him. But the Spook had drifted away to his private world. He was there smiling with his eyes half open, but that was all that was there. Sam looked at him close and saw that for all his loud clothes and bad color he wasn't a homely man or dumb in appearance. The fantastical parts to one side, there could have been some truth in the events he told.

Teacher-Man answered Shorty's question for him. "Maybe that Kaplin had two heads and he was laughing and crying at the same time."

"Well, was he daring or was he inviting, when he told Willie to bring some more with him when he came back?" Shorty asked.

"I don't think he knew," Sam said. "He'd been thinking two ways for so long he probably couldn't unscramble his true feelings himself. He needs a third head to sort him out. Of course, then *he'd* be riding a boxcar."

At that second, with a rattle-roar and swishing of air, a steamliner train went by on the next track. "That's it," Teacher-Man said. "We was sitting here waiting for that baby to pass. We'll be rolling now." The Spook's Mr. Kaplin was forgot, and Sam and Shorty and Teacher-Man scampered to the door to wish their hopes in. Sam noticed the Woman and Good-Rocking Poppa weren't taking interest in the prospect of rolling along and he looked back and saw them together in a corner of the car. He was pawing at her more than ever before and she seemed not to be pushing him off so much this time. Finally he caught her head in his hands and kissed her on the lips. Sam didn't watch any longer. He felt sick and disgusted at what he'd seen, thinking that there was nothing so ugly as a drunk fat man making up to a woman, unless it is a drunk fat man making up to a drunk woman tramp. He still stung where she had kicked him and he wanted to go over and kick her for using him as a tool to fire Poppa's jealousy.

The cars up ahead began popping and their car started jumping and they were moving again, at last. Shorty and Teacher-Man whooped and slapped at each other, but Sam couldn't bring himself to make any show of joy. He leaned on the door and counted trees — they were so scarce in the bloody hills they climbed over and cut through. But that got dull because the train made such slow time. The wheels that used to seem to be saying Maybe, maybe, maybe, were now whispering Birmingham, Bir-ming-ham, in a screetchy way that sounded like a threat. Sam knew his mind was the one really doing the talking and he tried to fight off the dread in him. All Birmingham was, was a big place where he'd sneak off the train and find another heading farther North to sneak onto. Policemen would be thicker than hoppy-toads after a rain, but a man who had got out of Lauderdale County ought not have too much dread over city law.

Of course, getting out of Lauderdale used up a lot of a man's get-up-and-go, and that was the trouble. Even though Sam had a bellyfull of this boxcar, especially the Woman and Poppa, a man wants to catch a breath between jumps. Even if the people around him are nothing much, if he knows he has nothing to fear from them, he'll tend to want to stay with them and will fear stepping out to what is unknown. Crazy as it was, the stinking hot boxcar felt something like home to Sam. The way he was thinking, he would have agreed to stay on it if it was going around in a circle.

But who says a man's life is supposed to be calm? Suppose he had been able to take pleasure in the slowness of the train that put off the time of coming to Birmingham, and suppose he had pushed the Woman from his mind, would he have had peace in return for asking so little? No, life don't work like that. For just then he saw a dusty red creature come running and stumbling full speed over a rise, heading for the train. He thought it was a runaway calf at first, or a big dog. He only saw it was a man when the man slid down the steep bank beside the track on his bottom. He clawed the gravel and was scarce able to stand up. He stuck out his arms to the passing cars and let his hands bounce off their steel ladders. Either he was crazy or was too tired to climb aboard.

The cars brushed by him and there was just one to go before the car Sam was on.

From head to foot clay had smeared his body. Waving and staggering there, he could have been a half acre of burnt-out land trying to get where it was raining. Or the ghost of a potato patch putting a curse on them for heading North. Sam wanted only to watch and not move until the car had passed by safe. But then he saw the fellow's face, his mouth stretched open to a crooked *O*, like he couldn't raise the strength to breathe. His eyes were red slots. Sam called to him and hooked out an arm to help him on the train. He caught him around the waist, but the fellow didn't help himself. He grabbed at Sam's face and shirt instead of the car, and the only way they kept from pitching off was by Sam throwing himself backward hard against the floor, dragging the other in with him.

They lay like a bundle. Sam had lost his wind and couldn't move and the fellow was out of his senses on top of him. "Great Godamighty!" somebody declared. "Where'd this come from?" They all stood around stiff and stupid, and Sam had to grunt two-three times before they had the wit to pull the man off him. He crawled free and sat panting for dear life. "What kind of creek-bed catfish have you done pulled in?" Teacher-Man asked, but Sam was still pumping wind up.

The fellow stretched on the floor, tall and scrawny, face down like dead. Nobody said anything for a minute, and then it was the Spook, even though he was wall-eyed and weaving and not looking much better than dead himself, that made the first worthwhile remark. "Look outside and see if you hear the dogs," he said. "Dogs? What you mean, dogs?" Poppa snapped at him scornful. The Spook bent down and scratched some of the clay off the man's pants, showing they had been white in color. "Nobody wears white canvas dungarees unless they're on a road gang. An uncle of mine showed me that. When I say dogs I mean bloodhounds." His argument was good enough to send Teacher-Man quick to the door to listen, and the rest of them glued eyes on him to wait for his findings. He leaned out and cupped his ear and looked into the far distance. His Sunday suit, riffling in the wind, made him seem to be acting a piece in a play. He turned and said, "I don't hear nothing." "Keep listening," Poppa ordered him, starting to take charge of things, the way he had tried before.

"I think we'd better get this guy in a condition where he can tell us the score himself," the Woman said and she rolled him over on his back. If the fellow had broken away from some prison road gang he must have wiggled on his belly — he was clay-smeared an inch thick, and the sun had baked the clay hard. The Woman dabbed at his face, then looked around for something to help clean with. Shorty handed her the whiskey jar, which still had a finger of moonshine left in it. "Who's got a handkerchief?" she asked and Teacher-Man tossed a blue rag from his pocket. She dipped and scrubbed for a good while, bending close to work on the man's skin. "Just pour it down his throat," Poppa suggested. "He'd choke to death," the Woman said and kept on working. Then she stopped and rared back with her eyes big and her lips puckered. "We seem to have us a white man here," she whispered.

He was, sure enough. While he had been beat down and sunburned to a point that somebody from the moon, maybe, would have argued if they had been asked to decide, he still had enough traces to get him by for white in the South. His thin nose and sharp chin were most in his favor. Otherwise, though he didn't seem to be very old, his crop of whiskers and close-cut black hair and the sunk shadow under his eyes and in his cheeks made him look more like a burnt match than any particular kind of man.

"He must have done something awful bad to get sent to a road gang. I didn't think they sent white men to the road gang," Teacher-Man said from his lookout post.

"Whatever he done, you can be sure he didn't do a crime against any Negro to get that harsh punishment," Shorty answered in a dry way.

"Well, now we know it, so throw him back," Poppa declared, strutting up and down and dusting his hand in the air to brush the white man away.

Sam had got himself bruised hauling the man in, and for sake of his bumps he didn't favor the idea of pushing him out again right away. "What for, throw him back?" he asked. "He's a white man all right, but he don't look able to cause anybody much trouble."

"Trouble? Why he's a regular Jonah," Poppa said. "There must be a posse and a pack of bloodhounds right on his tail. And when they don't find him, they'll remember this train going by and call ahead to Birmingham. A jillion cops'll meet the train — and what do you think'll happen to us?"

There was sense in Poppa's words, harsh as was the thing he wanted to do. This Jonah had luck in that he stirred awake right then. He would have likely awaked later eating road-bed gravel. He grunted and coughed and raised himself with his elbows. He looked around with drippy eyes and sniffed all directions. Sam guessed he didn't have any idea where he was and wondered was the whiskey smell a dream. "Take this," Shorty said, holding out the jar which was muddy inside and out with clay but had a little whiskey left. Jonah stretched his head out like a dog and lapped it up without putting his hands to the jar. After he finished he coughed and sat up straight. "You been put through the mill, mister," Good-Rocking Poppa said to him. "Yeah," Jonah said. "Where am I now?" Then he noticed they were all Negroes and he screwed up his eyebrows. Poppa gave a fat smile and pointed to Sam: "That bighearted fellow took you board this boxcar bound for Birmingham."

Jonah nodded blank-face thanks. He wasn't thinking so much of gratitude as of what they all were thinking. Almost always one white man among six Negroes, or a dozen even, is boss, automatic, because he carries the sheriff in his pocket. His word is law because the law always takes his word. But in the boxcar things were different; there wasn't no law, so numbers counted. Jonah seemed to understand that, woozy as he was, and was trying to figure how he stood.

Poppa played on Jonah's discomfort, tiptoeing around him like a big cat. "How'd you come to get yourself all dirtied up and tired?" he asked.

The white man answered slow and careful: "We were digging a trench for sewer pipe and the captain went into a roadhouse to get a beer, so I decided to see how far I could crawl."

"When did they start chasing you?"

"I don't know when the captain missed me."

"Then how come was you so all-fire pooped out?"

Jonah knew he had been caught in a lie. He bit his lip and decided to tell the truth. "I got about a mile when I heard a ruckus behind me and I jumped from the trench and cut out through the fields."

"Then they're right at your heels," Poppa said and his eyes traveled across Sam and the others. They understood he meant they should plan to throw Jonah off.

"How come you happened to end up on that road gang?" the Woman asked. Jonah took the question like a catfish at raw-meat bait. He saw she was giving him a chance to talk for his life. He chewed and swallowed and started his tale of trouble.

Jonah's Story

I'M A NOAH COUNTY man—that's where they had the big flood. They made Mudflat the county seat because it was the only part left above water . . . I used to tell guys in the army that when they asked where I was from. It isn't true, but they were always kidding me for being a cotton-picking sharecropper, so I would beat them to the joke.

Life in the County *was* something like being in a pond. Everybody floated the days away, big fish and little fish, moving past each other with a flip of the hand. They didn't have need to talk, because everybody pretty well knew everybody else's business, and nothing ever moved in from the outside to make a stir. Not that it was all sunshine and smiles; the big fish ate on the little fish—same as anyplace else in the world, I guess—but since none of the big fish was too big, they nibbled slow.

I was a Fluke. Harold Fluke. My buddies used to ride hell out of me on that, too. But Fluke meant something in the County. An old deed around the house showed that my great-great grandfather was the first white man to claim land after the Indians were chased out. We were a respectable family, except we had run dry of money. We had lived on rented ground all my life, not out of debt any longer than it takes a squirt of milk to hit the bottom of a bucket. The cow belonged to the landlord, the bucket was mortgaged and the milk went for interest. My daddy would sit figuring how much whiskey a week he could expect from the next year's cotton, since bootleggers were the only cash-and-carry merchants in the County. Mama would have the nigras out painting the side of the house facing the road — it kept spruce, even if we were wearing drawers made of sugar sacks ourselves. My sister taught school and went out on Baptist socials looking for a husband.

A family tree is like a greasy pole; once you start sliding down, you don't find any branches much support. It didn't help us none that a Fluke cousin was our landlord. Mama was always saying there were two kinds of Flukes, the Go-to-bank Flukes and the Gone-to-seed Flukes, and she had been tricked into marrying into the wrong bunch. And my sister said she wanted to get married to be rid of the Fluke name more than anything else. But we managed to float along and I would have likely floated along the rest of my life if it hadn't been for the draft.

In the army barracks guys from all over the country would sit around bulling about the big deals they were going to pull when they got out — becoming lawyers or taking over their old man's factory and stuff like that. Me, not only did I have nothing to say, but I couldn't even open my mouth without them funning me about my accent. It bothered me and I started looking at things like the GI Bill guarantee loans for ways of bettering myself. When my daddy died just before I got my discharge I felt almost glad, because it meant I would have free hand around the place and I had my mind set on a good Hereford herd of about two hundred head. I planned to borrow enough to buy them all at once. You got to think big to do big, they were always saying around the barracks.

Soon as I got back to the County I was itching to begin my money dealings. About ten o'clock of a morning I parked the truck at the courthouse square, still wearing my uniform. Then I got sidetracked by the sight of Jerry May Fluke standing in front of the old concrete water trough. She sprouted a wide welcome smile that really shook me up. She had been my dream girl, you could call it, when first I was old enough to think about girls — stirring me with her bold sex. And now she looked brash as ever, tall and slim in a pink sunsuit, her blond hair mussed up and streaked with peroxide strips. What's more, she stood stiff and pointed in a happy fashion, like I was a pool of cool water she was getting ready to jump into at a picnic.

She was kin to me, of course, a second or third cousin depending on how you counted, but we hadn't hardly spoke a dozen words in our lives. She belonged to the Go-to-bank side of the family and was three-four years older than me. I thought this welcome might be due to my uniform, but whatever it was for, I wasn't turning it down. We drank a Coca-Cola at the drugstore across the street, Jerry May and me. Squeezed up like we were at the little marble-top table I about busted my fly at being so close to so much bare-brown woman-flesh. She struck up a cigarette and slouched back to let me look. We talked about fellows I knew she used to run with. They were all moved away. "When are *you* leaving the County?" she asked tired-like. I told her I wasn't, but was planning on building up the farm. She puckered her red lips at that. "How come you want to punish yourself so bad?" she asked, but I saw that her eyebrow had cocked up interested.

"You still around, ain't you?" I kidded.

"I've been around so long I'm dry as old cotton stalks. There ought to be a draft law for women so *I'd* get a chance to see the world and have some fun."

I remembered she had started college some place in the East but got sick. She stayed for a long time in some sanitarium before she came back to the County. Her mama told people it was a touch of TB, and I had seen her looking pale and puny the last time I saw her before going to the army. But she looked fine now. "There ought to be some of the bright spots still operating near the county line to keep you from getting too dry," I said.

"Not if who you go there with is sawdust-dull," she answered, flipping ashes on the tile floor and letting her lids droop down over her big brown eyes.

I jumped on the hint and made a date with her for that night. I had a lot of parade-ground dust to wash out of my throat and some mustering-out pay burning my pockets. It didn't occur to me that even with the shortage of young folks in the County the percentage was all against a girl with her looks and money being left loose.

Jerry May went off to buy some finery and I went a few doors down to the bank to see Orville Fluke. He was about the same kin to me as Jerry May, and he and her were double first cousins, but I didn't think in any connection like that. I hadn't ever got more notice from him than a yellow fice dog—and his being the one to collect the rents off our place didn't make him good news around our house. I tiptoed up to the counter and asked the woman behind the glass shield that separates customers and money if Mr. Orville could see me. He was sitting right behind her, shuffling bonds or something. He looked up and waved for me to come around through the swinging door at the end of the counter and join him. He didn't pack much heft or talk loud and cuss — he stood you off by being hard-cold; cold as cash, people said. He had the makings of good looks, with blond kinky hair and straight-enough features, and he wasn't much more than ten years older than me. But he was drying out fast. His skin stretched tighter on his face since I had been gone and his hair was backing up and thinning out. This made his eyes pooch out heavy and purple rimmed.

I mumbled through my idea of getting cattle with a GI loan. He shuffled his papers some more then asked, "So you plan to stay in the County?" And without waiting for an answer he said, "That's good, carrying on in your father's steps. So few young people have a sense of family these days." He was a little young to be giving preacher-type advice. I let it go and asked if he thought the bank could arrange the money. He went on, "Your father was a real farmer. Almost the last thing he did was come in here and get a thousand-dollar advance on his oats crop so he could fertilize some pastureland. But then he died before he could get the fertilizer down or harvest the oats." He stopped, but it wasn't tears that stopped him.

I saw what his silence said, and since my mama had been running things slap-dash I didn't know any way of telling about the oats and the pasture. "He didn't pay you back then," I said. Orville just pooched his cheeks. "Have you got the note?" I asked.

"I lent it on his word. *His* word was good enough. But my cousin — our cousin — Jordan happened to be in the office at the time."

He had put it to me in a style that made me a son of a bitch for even thinking there should be signed papers, so I said, "Well, you can add that thousand to what it will take for the rest, if you can fix the loan."

Orville stacked his papers with a little shuffle and said,

"I'm afraid the government won't back up anything like you have in mind. It's all a lot of red tape. The Veterans Administration will let you buy a farm, but they won't help you improve it."

"Well then, could I buy the place we're living on?" I asked, willing to shift my idea a little. I knew Orville was bookkeeping the farm for his Uncle Carlton, who was in the dope-addict hospital in Kentucky. Old Carl had been gone a long time and I figured Orville would have the say-so on the land.

But he said, "There's lots of sentiment attached to that old farm. I don't think my uncle would want to give it up." He said it cool like he did everything else, with the heavy weight of the bank's money backing him up. Just the same I told him sarcastic, "It would still be in the family," and I started to get up and go. He flagged me back down. "It might be possible," he said, "to give you a standard bank loan for the herd — at eight per cent — if the other obligations are included in. You know, I didn't mean to say it, but your mother came a little short on the last rent. But the main thing is, are you really serious about your plan?"

I hadn't thought the interest rate would be more than four or five per cent. But since it looked like eight per cent or nothing, I decided to grab it. "I'm thinking big and I'm going to do big," I said. He gave me a fish smile and told me to come back when I had gotten prices on what I'd need.

I saw Orville again that night when I went by to pick up Jerry May at her house. He opened the door with a stiff question on his face and even after I explained why I was there, the question stayed. Before I got two steps inside the parlor Jerry May came gliding down the stair and hooked my arm to lead me out. "You all going to the picture show?" Orville asked. "No!" she said over her shoulder in a sharp fashion, leaving him standing in the doorway looking after us. I guessed he had eaten supper with Jerry May and her mama. He lived by himself catty-corner from them. They had twin white houses, both with big lawns and porches and fancy iron fences in front.

Feeling his eyes through the darkness made me uncomfortable because I had drove up in the truck — the only car we had — and it being used to haul cows and seed and stuff didn't make it very good for stepping out with a girl as good-looking as Jerry May. She really shone that night, too, in a blue dress of slick cloth that stuck close to her hips and waist and gave her bosoms the best of it. I apologized for the truck, but she just relaxed easy on the mangy seat cushion and said, "It gives lots of room in the back, don't it? You ought to leave some hay for a mattress." I was pleased at her not fussing and didn't put any meaning to her words.

We went to the Dixie Delite night club where, since it was a week night, we were pretty much alone. We danced in the long back room that had only the tinted jukebox lights shining. We drank whiskey — lots of whiskey. Jerry May could drink, by God. She drank the same as she danced, fast and hard, with her lips apart and her eyes distant bright. I wasn't accustomed to such a load of booze in so short a time and at the last my stomach was doing the jitterbug while my feet stood arguing. Then she suggested we drive down to the river and catch some air.

It did me good. A full moon on the white limestone bluffs of the Tombigbee, the woods smoky with night mist, and the old water moving along with silver light in the creases of its currents. The scene made me think of what was past: how, a long time ago, they used to slide cotton bales down the bluffs to the steamboats in the river; and of what was to come: how I would soon be one of those getting wealth out of the rich ripe land. I dared to put my arm around Jerry May while we sat on a fallen-down tree trunk, not meaning to try anything except hold her close, so that I could fill out my rosy view of things by feeling that I had a girl.

I got more than I wanted. She pressed herself against me, moving in between my legs and french-kissing and everything. When I would stop fingering her body she would dig her nails into my arms and back to spur me on. She didn't answer my sweet-words, she just looked off into the dark while she wiggled. Finally, when she had me fretted to a frazzle, we got back in the truck. On the road to her house she teased me about the girls I must have had when I was in service. I stammered and stuttered because I figured she was round-about mocking the dull style of my necking, and I promised myself I'd stay more sober and do better next time. I asked her for a date the next night and she agreed.

We went out together every night that week, doing the same as the first time, except I would come in from the country in the truck and then we'd change to her big black Buick, with her driving. I determined to make a better show as a lover, and what with her feeding my natural passion, I thought to try to lay her. Not in any smart-aleck way, you understand, but more or less to get a sure hold on her. I hadn't got my Hereford herd yet but I was already in my mind building a new house on the place for me and my bride, letting my mama and sister have the old house to live in. Me and Jerry May wore out that log by the Tombigbee, but if I wasn't in a fog from too many highballs while she looked raring and willing, well then she'd fight me; she'd let me feel and get close and then fight free, smiling but using all her muscle. Or else she'd tell me something that would near cause me to upchuck.

Jerry May knew lots of things which were rough and strange for a girl of her upbringing. If she hadn't been a cousin I might have learned a reason for her behaving that way. But the Gone-to-seed Flukes didn't believe in stopping anybody from making a fool of himself and the Go-to-bank Flukes weren't talking. Those people in the County who weren't Flukes of one kind or other just snickered.

I had been putting off a showdown with Orville about the loan, afraid in one way I wouldn't get the money and afraid in another that I would. Ten thousand dollars was what it came to, and that was heavy borrowing to think about, no matter how confident you are. When I finally went to the bank, Orville got up from his desk to meet me instead of making me ask for him. He talked about the weather and offered me a cigar. His face didn't loosen any, but I could tell he was trying to act friendly. The change in him didn't make me more at ease. He seemed to be giving away money that day, though. He didn't blink at how much I said I needed and the papers were out for me to sign in a minute. After the deal was over he said to me, "I hope you're about settled down to being a civilian now."

It was the first sour thing he had spoke during the conversation. I thought I could read in his face that he had seen me and Jerry May sailing off every night and coming back loaded. I had my money now so I talked back to him bold: "Oh no, the army didn't bother *me* at all." I was hinting at how during World War II his daddy had given him a farm to keep the draft board off him. And when they came after him all the same, he paid them to take nigras in his place. They might have got him at the last, except his daddy died and Orville took over the bank.

That night I was hot as an electric wire when I rang Jerry May's bell. Her mama let me in and I didn't pay attention to the turtle look on her face. She was of turtle build, too, with her short-cut red-dyed hair and round body. I sat myself in a big chair and acted like I was welcome. Jerry May came romping downstairs in a couple of minutes. Right in front of her mama she jumped onto my lap and began mussing up my collar and tie. I laughed and looked at her with the big question on my mind. I decided I would ask her when we were sitting on the log by the river.

But later we went swimming in the Tombigbee — jaybird naked, we were. She said it would cool us off, and I agreed, hoping to get more sober, too. I kept my shorts on when I undressed in the bushes, but when I stepped out she didn't have nothing on. She laughed at my shorts and reached to rip them off. I didn't want her to. She chased me and snagged them from the back, sending the buttons a-buzzing off. I turned, figuring she meant real serious sex, but she ran and dived into the water. I followed after, hardly able to stay afloat with all the whiskey and hot thoughts in me.

She took a long swim — it seemed an hour — even crossing to the other side and back. Then she stretched out on a patch of sand with her eyes closed, to rest up. Her flesh had the color of magnolia petals in the moonlight; her bosoms looked me in the eye; her mystery between her legs was like a dark valley inviting me. But there was in the tilt of her face a faraway expression which raised a picket fence. Not that I didn't try. I held her close, I fingered every part of her, but I couldn't mount her. She just slipped and rolled free. At last I was fretted into asking her to marry me, though it sounded phony proposing without any clothes on. She clobbered me good then, not even opening her eyes. "You're a little late," she said. "I'm going to marry Orville next month." That set me way back. I argued, not believing it, but she said it was so — it had been planned three months ago, before I even came back to the County. That finished me. We lay side by side, her a thousand miles off and me in my misery. After a bit we changed back into our clothes without any words.

When we reached her house in the Buick I was about to get out and ride off home in the truck but she grabbed me and finished scrambling my brains by running her hands inside my shirt and down into my pants, giggling because she knew I was beat beyond doing anything. At the same time, she said, serious and almost sad, "You're not such a bad one. I might be buying you yet." With the street light glaring into the car and all the eyes I knew were around, I didn't say anything, but ran away the first time she eased in her playing.

The next couple days I slept and stomped around the house like it was a cage. Finally the thought of the ten thousand dollars laying around doing nothing but cost interest got me up and out. I bought my cows — a real sweet herd — and some feed. But what I hadn't realized was how much the farm had run down. Playing around with Jerry May all the time I didn't get out to the fields. First off, I lost a couple head because the fences were out. I had to sell another couple to buy new wire — it cost too much to put on credit. The pasture sprouted mostly in devil grass and had to be plowed under. The oats had gone to hell. I was feeding the stock out of hand and figured it was costing me a head a month to do it. Then the market dropped out of sight; I could have bought two steers for what I had paid for one a month back, and calves were bringing steer prices. I saw myself sinking into a hole that'd be some time in reaching a mud sill. Plain enough I wasn't going to be able to make the bank payments. But damned if I would crawl to Orville asking for longer terms. I stayed out of town those days to keep from meeting him or Jerry May.

But the town started coming to me. After the wedding

had taken place and everybody knew I got took for a fool, people would pass by and jaw about things. They'd pretend I was a fence post and make private talk like saying the reason Orville and Jerry May finally got married was because they were the only two money Flukes out of the booby hatch who were breeding age. One fellow even whispered that it wasn't a TB sanatarium Jerry May spent all that time at. I had my grudge, but I recognized a lot of the gossip was pure spite. What kept eating on me was why had Jerry May let me go so far but not all the way. I still kidded myself that if I had really had her she would have gone against her family's plans.

Then bills started piling up in the mailbox. Bills, bills, bills — bills from storekeepers I didn't think could write. Our family always paid face-to-face whenever we did and with no reminders. What is more, they were figuring a ten per cent charge for credit, some of the stores, like we were nigras. I got the uneasy feeling somebody had seen I was going down and was rushing things by pulling out the plug.

Then one afternoon the big black Buick pulled into the yard and Orville stepped out. Jerry May was driving. You couldn't see her sunsuit straps from the house and you might have thought she was naked behind the wheel. I slung on a shirt and went out to greet them, puzzled and shaky. Orville said hello and asked if I wanted to take a ride with them, not looking me in the eye but keeping his gaze on the tin patch in our roof. I agreed, and we got in the front seat, him sitting between me and Jerry May. She could have never seen me before, the way she acted, and I acted the same. We ripped off about two miles on the asphalt road, heading away from town, then turned left on a clay road. Orville patted her on the bare thigh to indicate the turn and kept his hand there, his fingers wiggling and digging, after we had made it. His fiddling galled hell out of me.

We were headed for the Alton Fluke place — the old Alton Fluke place, I should say, since Orville had taken it over when Alton blew his brains out down in the New Orleans French Quarters. No house stood on the farm, it having burned down years before. There were just nigra shacks lined along the road. But behind, and reaching to the Tombigbee, was sweet, sweet land — light green pasture a ways, then dark green cotton in the bottom land, all trimmed round by river oak like it was a salad in a big bowl. We passed by four-five of the shacks until we came to one that had pink sideboards on it instead of red tarpaper. Jerry May jerked the Buick sharp to the right and pushed it across a ditch and into the yard beside the pink shack. If I had known she was going to try it, I'd have said she couldn't make it. There had been no rain for a couple days, but rain six months back is enough to make County soil like chewing gum. With the low wheel base on that big car I'd have bet good money we would stick till doomsday. But she made it.

Out of the shack came a colored fellow, a tall, stringy, yellow-skin man. He moved fast, then stopped in his tracks a good ten feet off to wait being called for. Orville ignored him, but got out of the car after me and watched me while I eyed everything. "How would you like to go in partners with me on this place?" he asked offhand. I thought he was making a bragging joke and said Sure, sure. He kept on talking: "I know you're having a hard time. Your trouble is you haven't got enough land to work with. You could graze your herd here. I wouldn't charge much for pasture and you could pay me that back from what you made by taking over these darkies and their cotton patches on a share basis."

Well, I just stared at the fields to keep from looking stupid, because I had no words, it was so surprising. The first clear idea to hit was that Jerry May had put him up to it. I glanced at her for a clue but she sat blank as a cow, not seeming to pay attention to us. Some little pickaninnies were gathered to admire the car and she might have been a girl in an ad posing for them. I asked Orville if he meant it. He nodded. "Both grazing and cotton?" I asked. "Both," he said. "It sounds real good," I mumbled, glass-eyed.

Then he called the nigra up. "Lonnie, come over here and meet Mr. Harry." This Lonnie joined us, his head bent respectful. I figured he was the boss-tenant, and probably a good one. He had a cool, steady air about his features, the kind of colored fellow that looks old and young at the same time. "Mr. Harry is going to be head man around here pretty soon," Orville explained.

When Lonnie heard this he raised his head and looked me right in the eye. He smiled and said, "That's mighty fine." But he kept his eyes on mine after he said it and his smile had sharp edges like the jaws of a monkey wrench. It isn't wise for a County nigra to be mysterious to a white and I was set back by him being so. I tried to read his reasons. His eyes, small and shiny, weren't unfriendly; they just peered right through me at something that made him want to laugh and pity both. He reminded me of my uncle who had caught me smoking when I was a kid. That uncle had smiled like that and then walked off, without lecturing me or telling my daddy about it. I didn't think this Lonnie had the right to put on such a manner, so when Orville said, "Why don't you two go look around?" I refused, saying I remembered the place from times when I had been bird hunting.

Jerry May came to life right then. "*I'll* show Harry around," she announced. "I'll show him some spots he might not have seen before." Her voice teased in its tone like she meant to take me out necking or worse. Orville's flat smile left his face and his eyelids flicked up and down. "Harry said he had seen all he *wanted*," he growled back at her dead and heavy. She made a big face and twitched her body disgusted-like.

That twitching brought doubts clear to my mind — it was like the way she had fooled with me before and showed she hadn't changed. The nigra had punched a hole in my paper bag just as I'd started putting groceries in it — now she had ripped it all along the bottom. Orville waved Lonnie back to the pink shack and headed to the car. I followed with some questions for him as he climbed in beside Jerry May. He clamped his hand on her thigh again and stretched back like he was about to take a nap after eating a full meal. I didn't see how I was going to make it on the old place, and this new operation might be just the booster I needed. But I was getting a little debt-sore. "I'd have to borrow for seed and fertilizer. How much interest would there be on that?" I asked.

"There's about four hundred acres good pastureland and the cotton allotment is twenty-six acres. You ought to do pretty fair right off," he said, misunderstanding me. I asked about the interest again. "Oh, about ten per cent," he said soft, his eyes closed in peace.

Per cent, per cent, per cent. I was making progress of one kind, anyway. I had graduated from eight per cent to ten per cent. It was then I remembered a smart-aleck soldier from Brooklyn who always used to say, "I'll play with your dice if you give me the percentages. Just give me the percentages."

I didn't have more time to think. No sooner had I shut the door than Jerry May started ramming the Buick around, trying to turn it to face the road. She rared forward, cutting deep slices in the yard, and stopped just short of the shack, flattening out a bed of sunflowers that grew beside it. She went into reverse and sent pickaninnies and chickens running for their lives. When she headed for the road I knew she wasn't going to make it across the ditch this time, and she didn't. The Buick flopped on its belly in the clay and laid there moaning and shaking. Jerry May kept gunning the engine. Orville popped open his eyes and said right off to me, "Get out and push." I told Jerry May to ease up because she was going to burn out the cylinders like that. "Get out and push, damn it," Orville said. I got out and looked for a board to stick under the back wheels to furnish traction. He hollered out the window, "Put your shoulder to the fender! Don't *stand* there, you bastard!"

He had no cause to call me bastard. I gave him a stiff look. He didn't meet my eye but was half smiling at Jerry May. I thought then he was embarrassed for talking to me like I was a cotton-chopper and I pushed a while, getting mud up to my ankles. I wondered why the hell Orville didn't step out of the car to lighten it. Finally I stopped and told him it was too much for one man. He reached over and snapped off the ignition to halt Jerry May's ripping and roaring. "Then roust out some of them nigras," he told me all impatient. I walked to the door of the pink shack and called. Nobody came. I went to the next and the next and called. The dark windows and doorways looked like faces with the ears cut off, smiling twisted and not hearing a thing. It seemed like somebody should have come out, since plain enough all that was wanted was a simple favor of getting the car out of the ditch. But I came back to the car with nobody.

Orville stood in the road. He was shaking his head and making sour faces. "Whoo, that's a real tough soldier boy for you, now. It's a wonder they didn't make him a general," he mocked me, but he talked more to Jerry May than to me.

I began to feel some sort of test was going on, specially when I looked at her face. Her eyes glinted bright, her cheeks were red and she wore a tight smile, like this was all a big ball game. Orville took charge, marching on the pink shack with his point-toe shoes digging deep in the earth. He yelled for Lonnie and got no answer. He stopped still, just like he was sensing the same creepy unfriendliness I had. Right then he stopped being a big man in my eyes. Big in a sly, dangerous way, I mean. From a rattlesnake he turned to a worm. He was hell-bound to get results, though, and he forced himself to the door. Before he could bang on the siding a woman came. "Lonnie's headed down to the river for some fishing," she said in a flat lie. I could see better than a mile down the path from the shack to the river and there wasn't a soul in sight. But Orville took it for gospel. Jerry May wasn't fooled; she gave a snicker that I would have joined in with if he hadn't tore into me then. "We'll try pushing it some more," he said, then *he* climbed into the car.

I pushed some more while Jerry May raced the engine wild. I could have suggested that we get some boards to put under the wheels and Orville would have listened, I think. But I was learning from those nigra tenants. I would do what he made me do, but I wouldn't offer a thing of my own free will. That Lonnie's smile reflected itself on the shiny blank trunk of the Buick I was rubbing my nose against. Except this time I grinned too. Orville *had* them. He was about to get me, except I smelled the rat in time. I vowed I would turn to rustling before I'd get deeper in debt to him.

A car drove up then. A colored fellow in a little Ford coupe. He was dressed in coat and tie and I recognized him to be the new preacher at the nigra Baptist church. He was coming from the woods, maybe from seeing a girl or a bootlegger or something. He pulled to a stop and smiled pleasant enough. "Mr. Orville, do you want me to tell the filling station in town to send out their wrecker?" he asked.

I couldn't see Orville's face, but his eyes must have been bugging out a foot at this chance to pay back the nigra people and square himself with Jerry May. "No!" he shouted from the bottom of his kidneys. "I want you to get out and push, you black — " And he called him a black-this and a black-that, all down the list.

The preacher took this abuse a minute, froze stiff with surprise. Then he clouded up and cussed back, sharp like a rifle going off: "Kiss my ass, you skinny white fart!" He stepped on the gas and started rolling on his way. I don't know where the man preached before he came to the County, but he had learned fatal words to say to a banker — and in front of the banker's new wife, too. The preacher must have thought this himself after he said them, because he drove like he couldn't see straight. He was no more than thirty yards gone when he wobbled off the edge of the road and went into the ditch, ruining his big farewell.

Orville sat breathing out big blue gasps of nothing. Jerry May was the first to speak. "Go get him," she spit at me, leaning out of the car window. "Catch the black son of a bitch! Kill him!" Her teeth were clenched, grinding together. An hour before, I might have rushed to the chase. But enough odd things had happened to slow down my feet and speed up my brain. I found myself on the sidelines, on nobody's team. Not that a nigra should say what he'd said in front of a white lady, but from what Jerry May had said to me on other times she didn't have the clearest of rights to get mad about what she had happened to hear. I didn't move. She glared, then gave me up and jabbed her husband with her elbow to prod him into being a posse. But he played possum instead. Maybe he didn't like the idea of being man-to-man against a desperate nigra out in the lonely country, specially when he knew he could wait till he got back to town and just pass the word for the man to be taken care of. So Jerry May jumped out of the car herself. "*I'll* fix him, then. If you *men* don't have the guts, I'll do it." She didn't look too rough and tough in her skimpy sunsuit and I tagged after her to keep her from getting hurt in case she did catch the preacher.

But naturally the preacher thought he was in for a real hunt and he did about the only thing a colored man in his fix could do — he took to his feet and ran. By the time Jerry May marched up to his Ford he was almost out of sight. She stopped and kicked the front tire. She didn't punch any hole in it, but what with the dinky sandals she was wearing she must have given herself a sore toe. She saw an old fence post in the ditch and started swinging it next, bashing the headlights and the hood and doing fair damage. Finally the post broke off in her hands and she stood heaving and blowing, a strap of the sunsuit down off her shoulder, leaving her near naked on one side. But she was pleased with herself. She figured she had shamed both me and Orville.

When her wind came back she blasted me. "Why didn't you chase him, you little chickenshit?" she demanded to know. I couldn't see how I had lost anything. I gave her a horselaugh. She flung the stump of the fence post at me. It sailed past my ear and I kept on laughing. Then she bent down and took a double handful of clay from the side of the road. She rushed at me with it and jammed it into my face. I was all unexpecting of this, and I got it good, in the mouth and eyes both. I scrubbed and spit — and worst of all, I heard Orville whooping with joy in the car. I wouldn't have gotten mad, I would have called it quits, if he hadn't cut loose. But he did, and I jumped Jerry May. It's not a proud thing to jump a woman, but Orville had messed up my dream that was dear to me, so I was going to mess up something of his. If that brought him out to fight I would fight him next.

I caught Jerry May by the back of the neck and jerked her over my leg, like the army judo instructors used to show how, and flipped her on her face to the ground. I sat on her back and pushed her face in the clay. She fought me, putting up a better tussle than her brother likely would have, and I have to admit I enjoyed it. Her bare flesh under my hands reminded me of the times I couldn't make love with her and so I made hate with her, sort of. I rode and spurred her while she carried both of us a couple of feet along the road on her face. Then Orville started laughing again. I looked at him. His mouth was open wider than I had ever seen it and he was bouncing up and down on the seat cushion.

That puzzled me enough to make me get off Jerry May. She lay stone still, not knocked out — her eyes were blinking — but listening to him. Then she rose slow and woozy, her sunsuit top hanging around her waist, and walked to the car, making two steps sideways to one forward. She went to Orville's side where he was still whinnying and hooting. She drew back her fist and told him to stop, her voice cracking like it came over a ten-party phone line. He leaned away from her fist but couldn't stop laughing. She threatened him with her fist for a long minute then let it drop. She turned toward me — bright blood on her nose, clay smears down her cheeks and over her bare bosoms — actually seeming to forget herself and be asking me for help. She looked pitiful, like a little girl that had dirtied herself in a sandpile and is fearful of a spanking. It was the first time she had ever *asked* me for anything. I took a step forward. But the look hardened quick in a flame of spite; she didn't resemble a little girl or even a woman then. I dropped my gaze and started dusting myself, not because I was afraid but for the same reason I don't like to look at cornstalks burnt dry by the sun. I walked home and didn't bother to get off the road when I heard the Buick roar up behind me. It went on past, mud daubed all over its back end, like complete strangers were in it.

That night, right after supper, the sheriff came by the house and said he was arresting me for assault with attempt to rape. He shuffled me off to jail and wouldn't even tell who I was supposed to have tried to rape — though I knew who had filed the charges. Still, I never did get clear the story Orville and Jerry May told. My lawyer was more scared than me and kept advising me to just sit tight. The judge had the courtroom cleared and he bent his ear while the two of them whispered their testimony in it. Me and the jury both stretched forward, wondering what they said. Jerry May wasn't wearing a sunsuit at the trial, but dressed all prim in a dark blue dress. She could have been Orville's twin.

But I was still a Fluke. Even if I wasn't a Go-to-bank Fluke, a Fluke counted for something. So the judge and the county attorney didn't think they should electrocute me like a nigra, which is what attempting to rape calls for. They changed the charge to attempting to ravish and dealt me fourteen years on the road. That was three years ago and now here I am.

"Three years!" Shorty declared when Jonah reached the end of his story. "What with your soldiering in the army, you sure have put in a long time in the service of your country."

"You wanted land of your own so they give you a bellyful of it. That's a real dirty story," Teacher-Man added as his try at a joke. But nobody took up picking on the white man. His troubles had a true ring to them. Good-Rocking Poppa, who had been hottest for throwing him off the train, kept his eyes on the roof of the car like he was hunting for wasps. The Spook had been nodding to show his interest while the story was being told and he kept on nodding in sympathy, though he might have been too dopey to understand anything of it. Jonah stayed crouched up tight. He knew they were sitting jury on him this time, and Flukes didn't count.

Then the Woman spoke up: "From what this man described I think he earned himself a berth on this Pullman. So I say, he stays." Poppa, without budging from his study of the ceiling, gave a long low whistle. "If he stays," he said, "we going to be all picking policemen's bullets out of our hides. He's a worse advertisement than a neon sign." Sam found himself agreeing with Poppa, despite Jonah's troubles. And he had a bone to pick with the Woman, so he said, "She likes white boys, you heard her say that. So it's natural she would want to keep him, if even the devil wanted him."

The Woman gave Sam a hard, pitying look. She shrugged her shoulders and spoke in a careless way to the open door. "You bastards that fear for your precious lives must have cow turds for brains. The cops are looking for this man, so you want to throw him off. But the cops don't know you're going to throw him off. If they are going to prowl this train in Birmingham, they'll prowl, and find you all whether he's on the train or not. It strikes me if you want to be safe, you better jump off yourselves."

Sam saw she spoke sense, even if she said it nasty. The policemen probably right now were getting together to greet everybody in Birmingham. If he was thrown off now, it still wouldn't be likely the Jonah would be caught in time to call off the search. Sam reasoned that the Woman was at fault for giving him all the time to tell his story, but since he had been the one to pull Jonah aboard he didn't say that.

Poppa, though, was bound and determined to get back on top. Sudden-like he picked up his coat, dusted it off and put it on. He did the same with his hat. "If he stays, then I'm taking a stroll. Who's for coming with me?" he asked, standing like he was waiting for a taxi to take him to some night club. He didn't get any takers, they were still thinking it over. "You coming?" he asked the Woman, making a pat at her rump. She just moved out of his way so he'd have plenty room to jump. Poppa shrugged and went to the door. He stood there. And he stood there. Even if Sam didn't like the man he could see his reason for holding back. The land could have been on the moon for all the sign of life it had; nothing but one hill after the other, getting higher as the train went farther, and none of them with grass enough to build a bird's nest of. No houses, no roads — and the bed along the track was steep and mean, promising anybody who jumped a sore ass, at least. Shadows were getting longer to show darkness wasn't far off, neither.

"You want a push?" the Woman mocked Poppa. He cussed at her and stood some more. Then he cussed at himself and sat down in a corner of the car.

"There ain't no place like home," Shorty teased him.

"And since we're going to stay one happy family, let's start playing together on this thing," the Woman said. "Who knows about how far it is to Birmingham?"

"I think we're near Bessemer, and it's ten miles farther on from there," Jonah offered real quick, smiling because he knew he wasn't going to be tossed off.

"There's not much time then. Everybody better start cleaning themselves up and put on some fresh clothes, if they have them. Right now, if we'd show ourselves the way we are, it'd be a gold invitation to the jailhouse," she said.

The Woman had taken over as captain, no doubt about it.

Right away Shorty began fumbling in his box of supplies, and Teacher-Man came up with a newspaper bundle. The Spook picked at the dirt and lint on his red shirt like he was taking pinfeathers off a chicken, and even Good-Rocking Poppa took out a handkerchief and dabbed at his face. Sam fished in his flour sack, too. Only Jonah sat still, looking worried and left out, him not having anything to better his appearance with. The Woman noticed that. "Look here," she said, "we're all together on this. But that man will be a gone duck in those prison clothes. Who's got something that can fit him?" Just the country men—Shorty, Teacher-Man and Sam—had brought any extra clothes with them. Shorty's couldn't be used, Jonah was too tall. Teacher-Man handed up a white shirt, like he was putting five dollars in a collection box. The Woman took it and glared at Sam. He pretended to be working on the knot in his flour sack, but she stared him out, and he gave away his number-three pair of blue jeans.

Sam thought then how strange this all was. Seven people running away from their worlds, caught together in a boxcar world: one white man, five Negro men—with a Negro woman of easy virtue ruling things. Every one of them, himself included, was an outlaw, and there wasn't no law in the boxcar. By all rights, a person could have expected rough trouble, but the most that had happened was big talk, a little drinking and some swapping of stories. Despite the lack of law they stuck together, keeping each other in line by pressure of sentiments. What's more, they had chose a leader on brains and guts—and maybe because she brought back thoughts of mamas back home. Even with his personal disliking of her, Sam had to admit the Woman had strength of will. It took a lot of the fear out of what was coming up ahead to think how people don't need a sheriff to make them people. Call them murderer or whore or nigger, they're still people. If the

North is free, he thought, it isn't much more free than this boxcar. He felt for the first time since he left Lauderdale County that he had something to hang on to.

Shorty, Teacher-Man and Jonah held their fresh clothes in their hands, but they crouched and bent their heads and didn't put them on. The Woman read their minds and laughed. "I'll go in the corner and slip on a dress, and I won't watch if you don't." She went off to the end of the car that was opposite where Poppa sat and picked up a flat cardboard box. Shorty and the rest kept the agreement. They held their backs to her while she unbuttoned and changed. The Spook was bent double, seeking specks in his pants. But Poppa had nothing to do, and Sam saw his eyes get like cream while he watched the Woman undress. Sam got mad, mad and curious both. He split between being honor-bound and wanting to show himself as careless of her as Poppa was. He turned his head and peeked.

He saw her in black silky pants and black frilly brassière. Nothing indecent of her body was showing, but that made her the more unsettling to watch while she kicked off the jeans and worked a slick red dress on over her head. Her neatness of shape was what got Sam. The line that marked her backbone ran from her shoulders to the beginning of her rump like a question mark at the end of a sexy thought and prickled his privates. The Woman turned of a sudden while she straightened the dress on her hips and caught him staring at her. She opened her eyes wide and put her hand across her mouth in teasing surprise and shame. Sam hadn't wanted to be caught and have her have something on him; he scrunched down real small and got busy with his own clothes-changing.

After a bit the Woman called out, "Everybody ready?" and they all said yes like it was a children's party game. She came back to the middle of the car and studied them. She looked like a cold flame in that snaky red. "Not too bad," she said. "Now what we have to do is do like the parachute troopers in the war. When we start getting into Bessemer we'll drop off one after the other, about a half mile apart, and keep on doing it when we have passed through the town. That way everybody has some chance and they won't catch us all at once, anyways."

"But what if they stop the train in Bessemer? What happens then to the poor bastards waiting for their turn to jump?" Good-Rocking Poppa asked, still trying to get back his lost power.

"I don't know," she answered him flat. "But if it'll ease your mind, we'll let you jump first." Poppa climbed down from his high-horse quick. She went on with her plan. "I think you better be first," she pointed to Teacher-Man. "You're young and can make a long walk to town easy. Okay?" He agreed. "Then you and you." She tagged Shorty and Poppa. "And you. Can you make it by yourself?" she asked the Spook. He was still picking at the lint on his clothes, eying each piece close, for all the world like a child catching fleas. He looked up with his face sober for the second. "I can make it," he said and went back to his game.

"You," the Woman said to Jonah. "You brought this on, so by right you should take some extra risk. You'll wait till we pass Bessemer — *if* we pass Bessemer — to go." He was willing. She turned to Sam. "I'm putting myself down as last. You come between me and the white man, if that's agreeable."

Sam figured that probably for spite she had given him a poor position, but he had his pride and he said, "Maybe I'll be the last one out." She smiled and shifted her body in a way that stirred the feeling she might be wanting to keep him with her and was planning in that direction. But he remembered what she was and how she had acted earlier, and he spit on the floor. She noticed that. Her face changed and she had hot words at the end of her tongue when things happened that made all the parachute trooping of no use.

The train hit a level stretch of roadbed and started going like billy-hell. There were mountains, real mountains, a mile or so off to the side, with long slanted wood buildings on top — mines, they were — but the tracks were in a valley. And shacks whizzed by thicker and thicker, to show they were getting near Bessemer. But they were going to go to Bessemer all together, because a man who jumped would tear himself to pieces. Teacher-Man didn't see this, though. He was a country man and he had his pride and he had his orders. He gathered up his package of belongings and stood at the door, waiting for the word to go. He was a funny sight, but a brave one. Despite the sudden speed hitting everybody across the face like a cloudburst at a church picnic, they gave a laugh that was like a cheer when the Woman put her arms around him and kissed him and said, "Let's wait a while, huh, tiger?"

They went through Bessemer so fast it was a blur of light, the street lamps being on although it wasn't quite dark. And the ground ahead stayed level and the train kept chewing up and spitting out the distance — if they were headed for damnation, they would go in high style. The ten miles to Birmingham would pass like nothing.

The Woman wrinkled her nose to show she admitted her plan was no good now. "You all better go empty your kidneys in the corner there," she said. "We're going to have to be traveling light pretty soon." Like schoolboys at a teacher's order, the men marched themselves over to take a leak. Sam could have used some relief, even if he didn't like being told to, and he started to join the rest. But the Woman put her hand on his shoulder and pushed him to get him to sit on the floor. He sat, from curiosity, and she sat down beside him, her face unreadable but her eyes quick and watchful like a bird's. "Everybody's been telling about themselves but you. What brings you here?"

Her tone of voice was cool and Sam feared she meant to make fun of him. So he tried to stall her off. He said, "I ain't got no story. Besides, the rules say it has to be about a white man, and no white man made me do what I did. I did what I did of my own decision."

"And you didn't do much," the Woman teased at him. Sam shook his head and made as to get up. She pushed him again, and this time slid herself closer, making her bosoms a barrier in front of his chest. "We haven't much time. Go on and talk," she said, just as sharp as before, but he thought he could feel warm blood running behind the ice, and it was that that moved his tongue. He told his story.

Sam's Story

THIS FELLOW Sam Cutler lived in peace for thirty years at the very same place he was born, living in close to the earth and not roving farther than he could hear the rooster crow. There is a pleasure in being nothing. He was nothing, and his mama and daddy and brothers and sisters weren't much more. They all of them belonged to the landlord, but the landlord wasn't heard to brag about it. Sam had been to four years of split-session school—two months before picking time and two months after, the term ran—but schooling hadn't changed him any more than manure can make flowers grow on top a rock. At thirty years old Sam was nothing, with nothing to be proud of and nothing to be shamed of.

When the baby chicken picks at its shell to get out in the wide blue world it thinks itself big and free, but come frying time, there ain't no shell to crawl back to. Sam didn't take that chance — he stayed safe in the hole he pulled up around him. Wanting to be something didn't help his big sister. She got to liking the movies they showed from a truck that would come park at the crossroads and she started singing movie tunes around the yard. So she was taken to town to work for the landlord's wife and sleep with the landlord. One of his brothers worried about the debts in the account book; he wanted to get enough clear credit to charge a hunting rifle, so he cleaned some land to plant some vegetables to swap. He looked such a good worker that he was swapped himself to a landlord across the county for a secondhand poison spreader. Hunting wasn't no good over there, either.

But Sam and a mule out in the field just moved along together like twins; he could have turned around and pulled while the mule guided, and nobody would have noticed. He ate his fill of food with no more griping from the rest of the family than if the food hadn't been on the table. He took his fun with women who everybody laid and it was no cause for ruckus or expense. In late afternoon times between supper and dark Sam would curl himself up in the front window and look. Looking at nothing down the path that led to the gravel road, just looking. Except sometimes there'd be funny cloud shapes in the sky and he'd tell his mama and she'd say it was God giving a sign. He never thought there was a message for him.

Then one day a white man brought word and the County School Superintendent himself was the man. He drove up just before noon and called out to Sam in the field. Sam let the ropes drop, because Jesse the mule wouldn't move unless somebody was behind clucking and pushing, and went to the fence. He thought it was somebody lost and he could point directions. But the Superintendent beckoned his finger to show Sam should climb over and come beside the car. "You Sam Cutler?" the Superintendent asked. Sam was so surprised at a white man knowing his name that he was ready on the spot to go to Parchman Prison or to take over as Governor up in Jackson. He didn't think how he was the only man his age for fifteen miles along the road. Besides the brother who had got traded to the other side the county, his other brother had been taken in the army and decided to stay there. And in both directions, the boys he used to play with had died or disappeared.

"I need a janitor for the school down there," the Superintendent said, pointing toward the Negro school three-four miles off. "It pays five dollars a month and you start work at four o'clock in the evening." Sam didn't have to ask if the Superintendent had the landlord's permission and there wasn't any thought of saying no, since they had his name. He became the new janitor.

The school hadn't changed from when Sam was a pupil. It was old back then to where it couldn't get older. With its tin roof and creosote sides, there wasn't much to rot or fall down. A washtub for drinking water sat by the front step and Sam supposed the big boys still took turns hauling it to the well down the road to get filled. Sam had been in school when the privy in back caved in. Its rotten boards lay in a heap and there was a path the children had worn since then, going out to the thickets to relieve themselves.

Sam had come early his first day to find from the teacher what clean-up chores she wanted. Though he knew the school he stood stiff and scared in the door. The job was what scared him — not the work of it so much, but the fact that he was to be the only one, the only janitor. He was being pulled out of his hole of nothing.

He listened to the children singing their lessons. Their

voices mixed together in the warm shadowy room, sounding like the hum of bees in a hive. He wished he could sit down with them at the two-by-fours on sawhorses they had for desks and their fruit-crate stools. But the teacher would find him out. He watched her moving up and down the middle aisle, going from the little kids in front to the big ones at the back, scooching past the pot-belly stove as she went. She was not an old woman, but her motion was bent and slow, and she seemed not so much to be listening to the reciting as looking out the window for something to come. He wondered should he disturb her, then he saw the Watcher in the corner. He had almost forgot Colonel Scruggs the Watcher, though he had been a boogie-man when Sam was little. He sat in his rocking chair sleeping like he always did, a little shrivel-up man with suspenders and string tie, but with buttons missing from the front of his pants. He had a doll look about him, a doll left in the rain and roughed up but that still kept its dead calm face.

The Watcher job had been set up twenty, thirty years back, when the white folks in town learned that somebody was adding up the charge accounts for the Negro families. This caused big stirs and arguments and one Negro man was shot and hung before the storekeepers found the schoolteacher was the one making the trouble and chased her out. They put in the Watcher to stop such foolishment in the future, and Colonel Scruggs was picked for the job from the start. He was old and used-up even then. He never said anything to the teacher or the pupils, he sat and slept; he might not have known why his sister brought him each day in a Model-A Ford and took him back home in the afternoon. But no child wanted to be the first to wake him up, and if a scuffle started the teacher just pointed to Colonel Scruggs to scare them quiet.

Sam was gazing at Colonel Scruggs when the teacher came

up to him and spoke. "You're Sam Cutler, the new janitor?" Her knowing his name was like the shock the Superintendent gave him and he listened close to her directions about sweeping out and setting the rattraps and nailing down some sideboards. The traps were most important because a child had got bit last month. She guessed that was why the Board of Education had decided to get a janitor. Sam rattled his head with each word she said, but she didn't look to care if he listened or not. She was tall and lean and long in the face, but the bend in her back never straightened altogether and her eyes stayed dim. Her skin was smooth and light brown, though he couldn't tell if that was from high breeding or bad health.

It took a while for Sam to stop doing twice the things he was told to do. At first he crept around the old school in fear of messing the teacher's work layout. Sometimes, seven o'clock at night, he would walk halfway home and then back again to school to be sure he had remembered to burn scrap paper, or a like chore. But soon he saw there wasn't any plan to the school's work — school started one day from where things lay on the last. He took to sweeping less and looking around more. He'd nose up to the map of the country that hung in front of the room and find Mississippi and wonder where in it he was, and why was it colored pink and the other states blue and green and yellow. He remembered from his school days that the coloring was just the way they made maps, but he wondered why they made maps that way. Thoughts like this led him to open the books left on the desks. The children couldn't take the books home because there wasn't enough to go around, and if one was absent two would be left without books that day.

Sam picked up a beginner's reader and did fine, with the pictures boosting him over what words weren't fresh to his mind. He read the story about the baby cat who caught a mouse with his mama's bandanna, but only held three corners of the bandanna closed and the mouse slipped through the free side. By the time he finished, it was dark and there were no lights in the school and he was hungry, so he set his traps and went home.

The next day he told Jesse the mule that story while they moved along the rows. But it didn't sound so funny on a second time. It for certain didn't answer no questions, except how not to catch a mouse with a bandanna. He stopped in the middle of a row and felt shamed of himself by name, shamed of Sam Cutler.

That afternoon he tested books till he fell sick. He started from the high-number books, the Seventh Reader and Sixth Arithmetic, and dropped back a number at a time after fighting with words which could have been upside-down for all he knew. He wouldn't let himself look again at the beginner's book. He gave up when it got pitch-dark and he left without touching the traps even. But in the morning, outdoors and with no books around, when things felt easy, he decided to settle on one book and do it through. He decided on a Number Four Geography, since he remembered it had pictures of people farming in it.

Sam read at the Geography. He read: "The Arabs live in the desert. They travel from place to place, riding on camels and tending herds of sheep. They are nomads." He did all right up to the last word. He puzzled that "nomads." He wondered if it was "no" and "mad" put together, but the picture in the book showed a fierce man wrapped in blankets who had a beard and a rifle. Then it flashed that they were called nomads because they lived in the desert and traveled from place to place. That was the trick: the last word added up the words that came before it. He read on about some other people and the trick worked again. He had solved two or three more when the daylight ran out. He walked home talking the new words to himself for fear he'd forget how he did it; he didn't eat supper to speak of, he curled up in the front window to chew his learning some more. It was in the moonlight, with the land and the sky almost the same shade, and nothing was moving, that Sam saw the key to reading. One word topped off a bunch of words, and then another word tidied off those top words, like stacking kindling wood, until you had finished the book and knew something. You had a neat pile of learning you could put to almost any use.

Sam finished his Geography. He stacked all the facts. He put the book down, real pleased at his smartness. Then the pile tumbled in his lap. He knew what Arabs and Eskimos and such were, but what was their connection with him? Somewhere in the reading of things he had missed the word that belonged at the tip-top. He decided to start all over again. He went over the nomads and this and that; he worked and stretched — but he came out same as before. The picture was clear of everybody in the world but Sam Cutler. Sam was out of his hole of nothing, with nowhere to go in its place.

Maybe the teacher had the important word, he figured. Since it wasn't in the book, her job was to tell it to the children. He plotted to get it. He punched enough holes in the side of the school to need his coming in the morning to carpenter, even though he knew he risked being missed with the mule if the landlord drove past the field. He tapped each nail in its hole easy-like so he would hear all the teacher said. But she didn't say nothing. Nothing except "You're excused but don't stay too long" and stuff like that. He couldn't understand why she didn't speak. He watched her drift around the room, hunched like a big bird. The bright little children shouted from their stomachs, "A is Apple, B is Book," and such. The middle ones were getting a dancelike beat in their reciting Two Times Two. The older boys and girls could hardly be heard, except when they giggled at one boy's winking at a girl, or something. Sam didn't see anything to stop the teacher from talking. Unless it was the Watcher.

Colonel Scruggs sat sleeping, of course. He didn't seem able to cause fear in a grown-up woman. But then Sam used his reading trick for the first time in plain thinking. He saw that Colonel Scruggs could be the top stick standing for the whole pile. The thought came that not only in land and crops and work but in their minds, too, the white people wanted a claim on the Negroes. It excited him with its great mystery, because what was the money and power in a Number Four Geography?

Sam decided Colonel Scruggs was going to miss school the next day, and then the teacher would be free to say her mind. He decided he was going to make the Colonel miss. He snuck past a cow-size watchdog at midnight to let the air out of the Model-A's tires, going through woods and brush to keep off the roads. When he finished his chore and lay on his pallet he felt like a catfish, breathing hard and wet with sweat. But he was at school for the start in the morning and the Colonel wasn't.

The teacher handled herself no different than before. She might not even have noticed the Watcher's being absent. Sam piddled around until almost noon and had made ready to leave when Colonel Scruggs was driven up, riding between his sister and another lady who was at the wheel. He recognized the car as the Superintendent's and guessed the lady driver was his wife. The Colonel's sister got out, but strange to see, instead of leading the old man she had to drag him. The fat old woman, her brown hair hanging flat from her head like it was pasted on, pulled her brother across the yard to the school door. His face was split all which way in complaint and he shed tears bigger than his head. She didn't waste time at the step, she heisted him under the arms and carried him, while he kicked, over to his chair. All the children in the school kept their heads turned away, but their eyes were peeking over their ears. The sister dropped him and left him, without his necktie on and not button-one done up on his pants fly. He beat his fists and feet on the chair and let his eyes and nose run.

Sam was outside the school looking in the window, so he was able to hear the sister say to the Superintendent's wife when she got back in the car, "Imagine. Even when he saw the children in the room he kept claiming it was Saturday and he didn't have to work." It seems the Colonel had got his days mixed up when the Model-A wasn't able to carry him to school at the usual time. It mixed him up bad, because two days from then his insides clabbered and spilled out — he just shit himself to death. But even though Sam had killed a man in his hunt for a word, he didn't stop. He planned to see the teacher at her house in private that Saturday night and ask her direct.

He picked Saturday night because then Negro people were allowed to walk the roads after sundown without question. She lived in half of a double house on the edge of town. The people living in the other side the house liked their whiskey, he knew, and they wouldn't likely be home. Which was good: he didn't want any idle talk started. This was to be a serious business visit. He didn't own a suit of clothes but he wore his white shirt and yellow pants when he stood knocking at her door.

Her voice asking him in was so weak that she had to ask twice before Sam felt he should open the door. When he stepped inside he didn't see her at first. The room seemed all shiny gold. An electric light bulb hanging from the ceiling shone on yellow wallpaper that had roses drawn on it, and made a smear of brightness in the big mirror of a dresser. The bed was of slick metal and had white sheets. This finery — the light, the wallpaper, the furniture — stopped him in his tracks like a torch does a bullfrog. He had to squint to find her sitting by the window in a cane chair. Her head was pressed close to the sill and couldn't be seen for shadow. She wore a lavender kimono.

"Oh, I thought you were my neighbor," she said and checked her kimono for gaps with her fingers. She moved her head a little out of the dark and he saw her face take the dim look it wore at school. She was itchy to get back to the window and he sneaked a glance over her head to see what was out there. He didn't see anything but the pink lights of the Blue Dahlia roadhouse.

"Is it something about the school?" she asked, since he just stood there. The best he could say was "It is and it ain't" since he didn't know how to ask right out for a word when he didn't know what the word was. "It's about you." She pulled back in the dark at that. "I mean, I want to learn something from you." But he hadn't made himself clear, because her body stirred and the edge of her kimono slipped and showed bare leg, bare all the way up her thigh. She tugged the cloth back in place soon enough, but he had seen it, bold brown under the bright bulb, like it was a woman's leg all by itself. He looked to his shoes, which he had oiled but they had clay from the road in the cracks now, and noticed he was standing on a red crochet rug. He felt he was crushing it and shifted his feet, but that only made the feeling worse. "What is it that makes you teach when you teach? How do you know what to say?" he asked her in a jumble of words, unable to stop the boiling inside him.

Her eyes shivered and sputtered in the dark, so close did they stay on him. They stayed a long time while blues tunes from the Blue Dahlia jukebox drifted in the room. Her neck muscles stretched tight and shimmied when she breathed and swallowed. "My home is in Laurel," she said in a sharp clear voice, not at all like her school way of speaking. "My papa worked in the post office." Sam nodded at that because it explained the niceness of her furnishings. "I am a Catholic. My mama was a very strict Catholic." He knew Catholic was a religion but he didn't see what it had to do with what he asked. He wrinkled his nose without thinking. She saw his action and bent forward, throwing her black hair so it covered her face. She stretched open the neck of the kimono to show a gold cross hung around her neck by a thin gold chain. It also showed to the light the biggest part of two breasts hanging like grapes on the vine. "You see," she said, "Catholic." And she straightened back again into the shadow.

Sam looked over to the stool in front of the dresser, trying to invite her to ask him to sit down, if this was going to be a long story. But she didn't. She went on about her life: "I fell in love, really in love with this boy. He was a wonderful guy, tall with a little mustache. He called me 'Désirée' and he really loved me, too. But he wasn't Catholic." She stopped and held her hands in front of her with the palms up, careless of how that made the kimono open up almost to her crotch. She tucked herself in and said, "He had two years to go before he finished medical school, so it wouldn't be practical to marry before then, and we put off telling my parents of our love. I was afraid it would kill my mama. Then the war came. The army took him as an officer, a medical officer even though he wasn't quite through school. And he came to our house in his uniform. Oh he gleamed in his stiff khaki with the gold bars on the shoulder. I thought then I would ask Mama if we could marry, thinking she wouldn't say no in face of his handsome bearing. But she wouldn't take me serious and I shirked from proving how serious I was. He left to go overseas, with us still engaged in secret, nothing more. Then, after a year passed, he wrote me from Japan that he had married a Japanese girl."

Sam had never heard of a Negro fellow who was allowed to study to be a doctor and he would have liked to ask her more about how that came to be. But since she didn't wait for questions he tended to disbelieve the whole story's truth. Talking fast the way she did, he couldn't help liken the high tone of her voice to a gramophone record. It seemed a put-on show, far off from the question he had come to ask. He glanced at himself in the dresser mirror to find some reason for this. He hadn't often seen himself in a glass that big. The mirror gave back a picture of a head muddy and storm-filled like a November cloud, and hands sticking long and hungry out of a white shirt. He looked like some jungle animal at a pool of water and it wasn't a pretty picture. He thought then the teacher was acting peculiar because she was afraid of him and he tried for words to stop her fear.

But she kept talking, rubbing her stomach and talking: "After that I almost gave up living. I didn't care for anything. I barely did graduate from college. Then I made up my mind to punish my mama, so I took this job here. I left home three years ago. But then my mama and papa got killed in a car wreck, and now I'm alone, alone here with no place to go, with no one to care about me." She stopped. She pushed farther back in the cane chair until all Sam could see of her face was her chin. It took a minute, because he was searching out her face for a clue to her true feeling, for him to see that she had spread her body out in a daylight-clear invite. But she wouldn't look at him and her fingers fluttered on the chair arms foolish-like, like they wondered what she was doing.

Sam reached up and turned out the light. She moaned in the darkness, starting to breathe heavy. He didn't know if to take off his clothes or not. The music from the jukebox at the Blue Dahlia came into the room louder than before. He had his shirt unbuttoned when he realized she had put herself by the window so she could listen to the blues songs. And he thought he understood the why-for of this sudden loving. She wanted to be low-down but didn't have the nerve to be. She thought herself too fine. He was a low-down thing in her eyes; the fancy lie she told about her life was meant to make him feel that way, and even when she pushed her sex right under his nose she still wanted it to be like she was being raped by an animal.

A month before, maybe, Sam would have done her the favor — it was free. But he had come with serious business and had been disappointed and insulted both. He buttoned his shirt back up and stood looking at her twist and squirm. He laughed to himself and walked home nursing a sneaky feeling of pride.

But the next day, Sunday, he woke up knowing he had come to the end of the furrow. The teacher didn't have but one thing to give a man, and he couldn't think of anybody who could show him the tie between what books said and what went on outside. He curled up in the front window and went back to his old sport of just looking. But that didn't satisfy. A chicken can't crawl into an egg. His mama came upon him from round back of the house while he was in the middle of his stewing. He looked up at the sky to find something to make talk about, but there wasn't a cloud in sight. She was carrying the chicken-feed bucket and the way she humped down he thought one of the fryers had got loose. Finally she said, "Old Colonel Scruggs is dead."

He said yes.

"He used to be landlord of this place before he lost it to the bank," she said after switching the top off a weed and some more fooling around.

Sam didn't know that.

"I expect he left some money even if he did have it hard for a spell."

Sam didn't want to talk about the Colonel, specially because of the stunt he had pulled on him. "Maybe his sister can buy her a new wig now," he said and shut his eyes to pretend a nap.

"She'll get the most of it, all right," his mama said. "There aren't any children alive — that *anybody knows about*."

He opened his eyes again, since he understood she was being mysterious. Her face had a twisty smile like he remembered from the time way back when she had stole a bag of marbles from the store to give to him. "What you mean, 'anybody knows about'?" he asked.

"There's *you*," she said loud and knocked his feet off the ledge. Sam's first thought when he could think was to look inside the house for his papa, but he was off fishing. "*He* knows, he been knowing, but he don't want to do anything about it," she told him.

That hit Sam funny, despite all. "And what's there to do?" he asked.

His mama had her plan. She wanted him and her to go to the lawyer in town and get a settlement. Nobody would dispute them or be mad. She knew three-four cases like that. The white folks just gave a share of the money and it was all over, quiet. She talked like she had been born to wait for Colonel Scruggs to die.

He told her he would go with her the next day but he wasn't meaning to. He was thinking how he had started out to find himself and had found out he wasn't himself. The school was a lie, the teacher was a lie, he was a lie. Only old Colonel Scruggs was true and he was dead. Sam decided he better do like the nomads — pack up and ride for some fresh ground. That night, before he left, he said goodbye by burning the schoolhouse down.

While Sam told his story the rest of the men finished relieving themselves and came and sat around. But they didn't listen too close; their eyes watched the outside flying by. It was solid dark by then, and Birmingham could pop up any minute. Only Shorty made comment. He said, "I think you were too harsh on that teacher-woman. She didn't mean harm, she just wanted a little co-operation."

"I wasn't in the mood to beat on my chest and play like I was an ape," Sam said.

The Woman pulled away from sitting close to him, asking dead-serious, "You decided you wasn't anything, so you left your home. Well, what are you now?"

"I'm not nothing, but I'm not an ape neither."

"What do you have to prove it besides a pair of pants?" she said and her scorn took in all of them running away in the boxcar.

Sam stuck to defending himself. "I got nothing to show, but I got it in my head. What I need is room to work out my thinking in, that's why I'm here."

"You going to get lots of room if you get up North. If

you're banking on earning your fortune with the contents of a Number Four Geography, you'll have miles of gutters to to choose from." The Woman turned on the others then. "Are you all just carrying the same old bones in a bag to bury them in a new hole? What are *you* going to do in the Freedom Land?" The early moon wasn't enough to cut the black shadow in the boxcar but she searched them out one after the other with her hot eyes. Nobody had a ready reply to dispute her with, but her rubbing it in hurt. So Sam came up smart: "If you mean we ain't got no profession we can make quick money off of, the way *some people* do, then you're right." Poppa laughed short and sarcastic to back him up. That hit her. She dropped her head like it had got nicked by a brick. Sam could tell from the motion of her shoulders she had started to cry, and his sharp answer tasted ugly in his mouth. He understood then she hadn't meant to be lording over them but was lecturing herself, too, in what she said.

Teacher-Man stood up and looked to come fight Sam, he was so mad at what he'd done. Sam would have let him pound on him, too, but Shorty caught Teacher-Man's leg and stopped him. At the same time, Shorty brought the talking back to the big problem by asking Jonah if he knew anything about Birmingham.

Jonah looked a lot better than when he had been pulled on board. But he was hang-jaw and too relaxed looking to be natural. It was like he had been wound up too much and his main spring had slipped and was running down. He took a long time before telling Shorty: "I been there three-four times. I got some cousins there."

"You think you might make it to their place when we get in the station?" Shorty asked. Jonah didn't say. Shorty went on, trying to make the white man do some thinking, "Seems to me that would be safest. Your kinspeople could hide you and if they had pull they might get you a parole, or anyways some money for a new life in another state."

"No!" Jonah shouted, jerking in pain from the idea. "I'm going North on my own, on the train. If I can't, it don't matter."

But Shorty kept jogging at him, despite his strong feelings: "Look, it ain't sensible for a white man to bum his way North with no money. A Negro man can because nobody expects him to have anything. But you'd be suspicious and likely be caught."

"If I'm caught I'll kill myself, that's all. I'll kill myself," Jonah vowed. His fierce mention of suicide went deeper than the rest of them were ready to go. Even if he was only talking rash on account of his being too beat up to want to stir any more, he still made a ripple that splashed all around. They expected trouble in Birmingham — maybe arrest, beating, jail, maybe shooting, maybe death. But those were things that had happened to other people, and so they could expect them for themselves. Not expect in any happy fashion, but be prepared for and try like hell to miss. None of them had thought of anything so bad they'd kill themselves over. It started them imagining what *that* could be and was unsettling.

Poppa broke the mood with a nasty crack. "Go on," he told Shorty. "Persuade him to move in with his cousins. He can tell them he's an animal trainer for the circus, and we'll go along as his pet monks."

The Woman stood up. She had her tears stopped and with a stiff look at Poppa she took back command of the boxcar. "*Somebody* better be making up their mind to stay in Birmingham," she said. "Maybe all of us better be. Unless, maybe, a decoy might do a trick that'd save the rest of us." It stirred their spirits to learn she had some plan in mind, but hearing that a goat would be needed to make it work gave it a scary edge. "Well, we been listening to each other talk for quite a time now. So which one of you sinners has decided that his life is worth less than the rest's?" she asked and giggled low in her throat.

They rode along silent. Then Teacher-Man pointed out the door to the mountains that were twinkling with the glow of houses and showing how big was the city. "There's a statue up there. A man holding a red light. What the world is that for?" "It's a popsicle he's holding," the Spook guessed. "That's Vulcan, the man of iron. He's the Birmingham mascot," Jonah said, without needing to look at the thing perched on the mountain top. "I bet it's a club he's got in his hand," Shorty said. "He's waiting to smash down the people if they try to claim their rights."

"We're in, then," the Woman said. "If the train slows down and there's a clear spot, don't talk, just jump." But she herself didn't crowd the door, showing she didn't believe there would be much chance for that.

The train slowed. Its turning off the power and starting to coast felt to Sam like his heart had stopped to beat and his lungs were locked. "There's wire fence and spotlights out there," Teacher-Man wailed. "Let's try to shut this door, anyway," Poppa said in a desperate voice, starting to push on the sill. "That won't keep nobody out. It'll just lock us in," the Woman said, stopping him. They sat rolling into the freight yard, like cows going down a slaughterhouse chute.

What Happened in Birmingham

THE TRAIN shuffled to a stop and they found themselves looking out at the sheet-metal side of a warehouse that shone like silver in the round circle of light from a goose-neck street lamp. The air shimmied with fog and smoke, and the pavement beside the track looked like old rotten bone. It was a dramatic place, a real play stage, for them to win or lose in. They lined up, one back of the other, on each side the doorway, pressed flat against the car wall. Sam was behind the Woman and behind him was the Spook. The rest were on the other side.

In a minute's time they came — city policemen and railroad policemen, six of one and two of the other. They all had on dark blue and were red-face. The city police wore beak caps, the railroad men white-brim hats. They made heavy walking sounds on the pavement and bounced the train engineer along in front of them like they'd have just as soon stepped on him. The engineer was a tubby old man in overalls and high hat. He was making his complaint, though. He said, "Now you guys understand this train is thirty-two minutes late already. If we lose any more time we'll get into Atlanta after the switching crew has gone off and there'll be hell to pay."

They stopped right in front of the boxcar. "Okay, pops," one of the city police said. "We'll make this fast. Harry, you and three of the guys go quick to the end of the train and start combing forward. I'll take Mac and the two railroad snoopers with me and work from front to back. I'll change their diapers if any shooting starts." They all laughed big at that, then pulled out big black pistols and moved off to the search. The engineer scratched his head and trailed back to his engine.

Word that the train was going to Atlanta, and soon, froze the people in the boxcar more than knowing that the hunt was on. Like a bunch of grapes hanging beyond their fingertips, they saw that if the police should miss them, all they'd have to do was sit pat and whistle goodbye. If they missed them.

The Woman whispered, her breath popping with whip-sharpness, "We need a decoy, *now.*" Nobody even let their eyes blink for a second there, not wanting to lose their seats on the Georgia Express. Then from behind Sam the Spook moved up to beside the Woman, his head hunched down and his rump stuck out to imitate a football player. "What you want done?" he asked. "Are you sober?" she asked back. "Goddamn, if you were looking for a priest to do the job, you should have said so," he snapped. She gave in and described her idea: "Climb underneath the car and crawl the ties fast as you can and get ahead of those bastard cops that are walking toward the engine. They're going slowest. When you're about to the end of the train, cut out into the open and look for a gap in the fence to get through. Maybe there'll be one, but I wouldn't bet on it." The Spook straightened up and clicked his heels and swung his hand in a big salute to her. Then he was gone over the side, slicker than an eel.

The seconds passed by, marked by the heels of the policemen on the pavement, without a scrape or scratch to tell how the Spook was doing. If a stick of dynamite had been lit and nobody knew where it was or how long a fuse it had, there couldn't be a worse feeling. "I bet the son of a bitch is just sitting down there hoping they don't see him," Good-Rocking Poppa said.

"Do *you* want to go down and find out?" the Woman asked him. She whispered to Sam real shaky: "I didn't tell him to be sure to run out the side the train opposite the cops. I didn't tell him because I wanted to be sure they'd see him and have him lead them away from us. He's smart enough to think of that for himself, he'll think of his best chance. But I know the sweet sucker won't take it; he's going to make a target of himself. And I sent him."

She gripped his hand and more seconds passed. Then Hey!

the shout came from down by the engine, followed by Blooey! Blooey! Blooey! In her plan the Woman had forgot how far policemen could shoot. "I got the mother-kicker!" the shout came. And from the tail end of the train a policeman yelled, "Did you get him, George?" The George policeman called back, "I got something, but it looks like only a nigger." They didn't even gather together to peer at the body. One of them said, it must have been a railroad policeman: "I better call a redcap to haul him off. We don't want the Board of Health closing down the line." They started their search of the cars, moving from both ends to the middle, some on each side of the train. Old Spook had made his try for nothing and wasn't going to get another one.

Scrunch, bang! Scrunch, bang! They slammed open the doors of a car and slammed them shut again. Clomp, clomp, clomp. They moved to another one and opened and shut it, drawing closer to the people in the boxcar. From the sounds Sam tried to guess how far off they were and what party of policemen was the closest. Like a fish in the bottom of a boat he blew a big breath with each door slam.

The Woman spoke in a loud voice that made them all jump. "You fellows back up from the door and stay in the shadow. Don't follow me now. Stay hid. Except *you*, you're coming with me." And she gave Sam a smile of scorn and leapt off the car onto the pavement, pulling him along behind her by the hand. He was too surprised to put up any arguments.

The warehouse roof eaves cast about two foot of shadow, and between it and the pavement ran a little strip of crabgrass. She towed Sam there and while he was still wobbly with astonishment she faced him, grabbed his shoulders, and by her kneeling and tugging they ended up with her flat on her back and him belly-down on top of her. She spit cuss words and sex words at him, her lips drawn tight and showing her teeth. He thought she had lost her mind. He raised himself somewhat and shook his head no, and dug his toes in to get free and run. But she caught his clothes and her legs spread out and locked around his waist. He stayed with her. He stayed, scraping and wiggling like a rat burrowing a nest in the straw of a jailhouse floor.

The policemen's steps were growing closer. There was no doubt of their being seen any second. But the clomp-clomp-clomp of heels bounced off the two of them like they were wrapped up in a bullet-proof blanket, up in the air or under the ground, invisible to sight. The Woman kept whispering him words and Sam jerked like a dolly on a string. She gave him a smile of mocking mixed in with a tenseness that cut deep hollows in her face. She had him at her mercy. His eyes were closed; his kneebones plowed at the concrete, but he didn't seem to feel.

"For Chrissakes, what's that?" a policeman yelled. They had been seen. "It's a nigger man and woman, lying here drunk and screwing up a storm. Come see, Harry. Hey, the rest of you guys, we got something rich here."

From both directions and both sides of the train they came dog-trotting. "Man and a woman screwing, eh? Step out the way, Mac. I'll show you my billiard shot. It ain't often you get a chance to do in two of the black monkeys with one bullet."

"No, George, let 'em go on some more. Let's watch," the man who had found them pleaded. Then he poked Sam in the back with his pistol. "Come on, nigger-boy, get hot," he said.

Sam didn't look up or show notice, but so many things burnt at him — fear, shame, sex — he fired inside like an electric bulb and it was like being able to see through his skin what went on behind him.

All eight of the policemen had gathered around, guns in

hand, making a thick blue fence. Their bent-over faces cut off all light except that which reflected red and raw off their skin. The air turned butter-thick with whiskey and sweat smell.

"Too bad we ain't got no gasoline to pour on them."

"They sure have nerve. Right here in the station."

"It wasn't nerve. They're just like animals. They wanted to, he gave her two-bits, and so they did it at the closest spot."

"I don't know if he bought this for two-bits. She's not a bad-looking piece for a nigress."

"No, not at all bad."

"I'd still like to put a slug right down through his pecker into her belly. That'd give them a charge, that would."

"Aw, George, you're just jealous 'cause you can't do it with your old lady any more."

They laughed at George. Then they fell silent and edgy. Sam knew their minds had turned to lusting after the Woman. If she was by herself they would have spread her out and taken turns, that's what they were thinking. But he was there and none of them wanted to be first to suggest taking seconds after a Negro man. That ate their pants and Sam was sure that in a bit more they would join with George in doing spiteful harm.

And then another man walked up. "The engineer wants to know if he can drag on out now," he said. "What? Oh sure," the George policeman answered. "The convict ain't on this freight." The new man gave a hand signal and right away the train rattled and coughed while the engine started tugging against the cars to get them rolling.

Sam saw for the first time that this love-making was the Woman's plan to make the policemen neglect to look in the boxcar where the rest of the people were. The wildness of the idea, and its working, hit him like a bucket of cold water.

Good-Rocking Poppa, Shorty, Teacher-Man, Jonah were all saved, but he was left trapped to be tortured by the white men. He wanted to pull himself loose from her and cry out and holler and beg for his life. He was ready to tell where the others were in order to turn the policemen's attention from him. He was ready to betray.

Then he looked into the Woman's face, meaning to spit at her. Her eyes were shut, not clenched shut, but with the lids smooth and calm and sure. Coolness made a clear light on the ridges of her cheeks and nose. Her bangs lay on her forehead, in neat curls despite what all, like a queen's hairdo. He felt strong and weak in the same second. He wrapped her in his arms and lay there, ready for anything that would happen next. What happened was like a dream.

"What's that there?" the new man asked the policemen after he finished signaling the engineer. "Ain't you old enough to tell?" one of them answered in mean fashion. But the new man stuck at it. "Well, what you all meaning to do?" he asked again. His voice had a tone that showed he read their minds pretty good and didn't like what he saw. He got no answer. So he said, "I guess I'll have to throw them out myself then, if you fellows don't feel it your job. I don't recollect any regulation against what they're doing, but it's not making any money for the company, so I better get them off company property. That dead man out there hasn't got a shipping tag on him, neither, and he better be moved. How about you guys doing that, though, huh?"

The policemen gave way to his wishes. The new man tapped Sam on the shoulder. Sam stood up quick and caught the Woman under the armpits to rush her to her feet. "Come on, buddy, you and your girl friend have to shove off," he said flat and dry. "Yessir," Sam agreed. The Woman was weak and he had to hold her by the waist. While the three of them walked along, Sam sneaked a look at the new man. He was no bigger than a watch fob, a gray old man with thick glasses. He had on a dark vest and arm-garters, the old-fashion way railroad people dress, and Sam figured he was a package checker or some such. He kept his eyes straight ahead, showing no curiosity for them, and Sam understood he shouldn't thank him out loud.

Sam didn't reason it through till a long time later, but he came to think how that railroad man's manner showed how a white man who doesn't like to see Negroes beat and killed can stop a good bit of it, and do it easy. He can just make it known he is ready to be a witness. He might not ever have to raise his hand and swear, he doesn't have to give a helping hand in big style. He just needs a steady eye. A Negro can't be a witness. A policeman won't tell on another policeman. But the tiniest white man can shame off murder and bloodshed if he looks on and hints by not joining in that he doesn't agree. It is a cruel time when policemen have to be policed on, but it is true.

They walked the same direction the train was pointed and it happened that the train got rolling the same time they did. The old boxcar went by, dark and empty-looking. Sam felt like somebody was driving off with his mule. Then when the car reached the end of the warehouses, about a hundred feet past the Spook's body, he saw his sack of belongings and the Woman's box dropped off. An arm stuck out the car door. Its hand waved a goodbye then clenched into a fist of gratitude and of wishing luck. Sam couldn't tell whose arm it was that risked policemen's eyes to make the sign. Because of the distance and the darkness there was no choosing whether the arm was black or white. Shorty, Teacher-Man, Good-Rocking Poppa, Jonah — but it didn't matter who. It was a danger to them all and a salute from them all, Sam recognized.

The package checker marched them past the Spook, past their belongings, all the distance to the COLORED ONLY passenger waiting room, taking them to where there was light and people, doing the favor without showing it was a favor. He stopped at the screen door. "Get going," he said. "Get going." Sam thanked him with his eyes and the white man fiddled with his gold pocketwatch.

They were a mess, Sam and the Woman with their clothes scuffed and wrinkled ever which way, and the half-dozen people in the waiting room got on their toes to stare. The Woman found her strength, though, and they stepped fast through the room and out the front door to the street.

"Let's get a beer, how about it?" the Woman asked, smiling easy and pointing to a blue-lit sign a half-block off in the middle of a bunch of dark buildings. "Too close," Sam said, having the policeman in mind. But he let her pull him there, seeing that her bossiness was strong as ever. And he didn't ask how she knew it would be a barroom for Negroes, he just walked in after her. The bartender and the ramblers around the bar gave a big eye, like they figured out what the two of them had been doing, but went back to their own business. Sam didn't think they guessed how far they had come. The Woman slid herself atop a stool like a duchess and he hobbled up, too. She reached in the bosom of her dress and came out with some dollar bills fastened by a hairpin. "Two beers," she said, slapping the money on the bar. "And a glass of ice water," Sam said.

They got the beer and a glass of ice water each. He choked the water down and asked for another. She sipped at the beer and then went after the water, too. "Those poor boys on the boxcar could sure use some of this," she said. "They got their freedom to whet their chops on," he said. "Who ain't free?" she asked and smiled like she had a secret treasure. She turned herself to patting bits of her hair back in place and picking at her dress. Without stopping primping she said, "Well, how did it feel?" Sam pretended he was trying to pour his beer without getting too much foam on the glass. "How did it feel?" she asked again, her voice like barbwire.

Sam sat there eating all the dirty cracks he'd made about her having been a whore. Not more than fifteen minutes ago he had been sporting in public as much as any two-bit woman could do, yet he hadn't lost his pride. This wasn't exactly because it was different with a man than a woman; he had done what he did for a reason — even if he didn't learn the reason till late. He saw that what a person did because he had to didn't have direct connection with his pride; if his pride could make something of it and keep alive, it didn't matter what he did.

And farther back in his past, Sam felt sorry for the way he had shamed the teacher-woman whose pride he didn't understand, but whose pride was so big she didn't know how to do anything. And his mama. His mama was only trying to catch something back for the wrong done her a long time before; she hadn't meant to hurt him, Sam . . . "Will you marry me?" Sam found himself saying out loud to the Woman.

"Of course," she said. "Now slip back to the freight yard and get our baggage where the boys threw it."

Sam fetched their things. They rented a room in a hotel. He wanted to sleep for two days, at least, to get the kinks and knots out of his carcass, but the Woman rousted him up early in the morning and made him go with her to sell a gold locket she had carried in her possessions. After that they took a taxi to the county morgue and claimed the Spook as their brother. By the time they had paid this and that fee, and bargained with the undertaker to do a burying job reasonable, there wasn't much left of the locket money.

The Woman asked Sam, "What time is it?" He looked up to gauge the sun. The sooty air and tall buildings got in the way, but he kept squinting. She laughed and jabbed him in the ribs. "Over there, country boy," she said and pointed to a big clock stuck up on the roof of a filling station. It read one-thirty. "The City Hall must still be open, so let's buy a wedding license and finish up that chore," she said.

He had seen enough money paid out on official business and foolishment for one day, though of course the Spook deserved what they had done. It wouldn't have been right to leave him in the hands of the policemen, even dead, since the rest of the party had made a getaway. But thinking of more hard-face white clerks to be polite to and hand dollar bills to, made him tired. "Ain't it kind of unwise to spend on more formalities since we're riding so close to the rim now, and with no prospects in sight?" he complained.

She looked him over hard, stopping right in the middle of the busy sidewalk. "If you're waiting on prospects to get married," she said, "you going to be too old and cold to enjoy it. I don't want to marry you because we've got something. I want a marriage that'll do something. But I can get along on my ownsome. God knows, chasing after you wasn't the best idea I ever had."

So they got married, with a license and a preacher, and even a steak dinner afterwards.

Sam found a job as janitor in an office building and his wife took work — not doing what she used to — but teaching in a grammar school. He checked on the map and found he had only traveled a hundred and eighty miles on that long train ride from Lauderdale County and that explained to him why there was foolishment like separate elevators for white and Negro in buildings and a city law saying a white man and a Negro can't play checkers together. But at the same time Birmingham had more Negro people and that was a difference. Because there were so many Negro children, Sam's wife could fib a few facts about herself and get hired to teach. At a cut rate, of course. Because there were so many janitors and porters and handymen like Sam who wanted to learn to do something else, big promoters could set up places to teach welding and such at night. At a price. More than that, a Negro man could get the vote if he had the money for poll tax, because there were Negro lawyers to go with him to see that he wasn't beat up or shot.

Sam and his wife live by the train tracks in a long row of old bungalows. The trains go by and shake the walls and rattle the dishes, and they laugh. For her, there is going to be the trouble when the white folks have to be shown that the Negroes want one and the same schools for everybody. Sam, when he gets good enough with the torch, plans to knock hard on the door of the building workers' union. They aren't in Birmingham permanent, they know, and their joke together is that maybe on their next freight ride they'll get as far as Atlanta.